OCT 15 1996   SOCV

P-1-ARI-830

D0122658

Teens & Tobacco

A FATAL ATTRACTION

Susan S. Lang and Beth H. Marks

3 1336 04067 4427

TWENTY-FIRST CENTURY BOOKS
A Division of Henry Holt and Company
New York

Twenty-First Century Books
A Division of Henry Holt and Company, Inc.
115 West 18th Street
New York, NY 10011

Henry Holt® and colophon are trademarks of
Henry Holt and Company, Inc.
Publishers since 1866

Text copyright © 1996 by Susan S. Lang and Beth H. Marks
All rights reserved.

Published in Canada by Fitzhenry & Whiteside Ltd.
195 Allstate Parkway, Markham, Ontario L3R 4T8

Library of Congress Cataloging-in-Publication Data
Lang, Susan S.
Teens and tobacco : a fatal attraction / Susan S. Lang and
Beth H. Marks. — 1st ed.
p. cm.
Includes index.
Summary: Discusses the effect of smoking on teenagers and why they smoke.
1. Teenagers — Tobacco use — United States — Juvenile literature.
2. Tobacco habit — United States — Juvenile literature.
[1. Smoking. 2. Tobacco habit.] I. Marks, Beth H. II. Title.
HV5745.L35 1996
362.29'62'0835 — dc20   95-40738
                                                              CIP
                                                               AC
ISBN 0-8050-3768-3
First Edition 1996

Interior design by Kelly Soong
Charts by North Market Street Graphics

Printed in Mexico
All first editions are printed on acid-free paper ∞.
10 9 8 7 6 5 4 3 2 1

—〰—

For all the kids who have the good sense and personal strength to stay tobacco-free

—SSL

For my mother, who would have been pleased

—BHM

ACKNOWLEDGMENTS

We thank those who helped us find teens to interview, including Dr. Ray Graham at Harrison County High, Kentucky; Dawni Nelson in Las Cruces, New Mexico; and Pepper Koalan and others who helped SSL on-line. Many thanks to the kids who were willing to tell us about their lives and why they smoke. We are also grateful to Dr. William Cahan, who reviewed the manuscript and provided valuable comments and information. Our daughters, Julia Schneider and Libby Marks, were cheerful and reliable couriers.

SSL: Special thanks go to Tom Schneider for his enduring love and support; and to Sol Lang, whom I have not thanked enough.

BHM: Thanks to Peter Marks for his encouragement, insight, and love, and to Peter, Anna, and Libby, who tolerated a large mess for a long time.

CONTENTS

Profile
ART   7

1
TEENS AND TOBACCO: AN OVERVIEW   9

2
HOW DID WE BECOME A NATION OF TEEN SMOKERS?   14

Profile
ALEX   26

3
WHY TEENS SMOKE   28

Profile
MARY ROSE   37

4
**HOW CIGARETTE ADVERTISING SEEKS CONSUMERS
AND SEDUCES TEENS**   39

Profile
GABE   56

5
WHY THEY CALL THEM "SICKARETTES"   59

Profile
BRANDON   73

6
**BIG BUCKS UP IN SMOKE: THE ECONOMIC
COSTS OF SMOKING**   75

Profile
CATELYN   84

7
**HOW SMOKING IS LOSING ITS COOL: SOCIETY'S
CHANGING VIEW**   87

Profile
MATT   101

8
TOBACCO: AN INDUSTRY UNDER FIRE   103

Profile
TORY   114

9
KICKING THE TEEN TOBACCO HABIT   116

Source Notes   125
Index   142

Art
A Typical, and True, Story

"I was eleven the first time I smoked," recalls Art, a forty-five-year-old accountant and father of three. "A neighbor who was several years older offered me a cigarette and showed me what to do with it. I inhaled, and I think I passed out!"

Despite his startling first experience with smoking, Art was smoking almost a pack of Chesterfields a day by the time he hit junior high. "It was part of being cool and hanging out." Art's father, a regular smoker, had just recently died of a sudden heart attack. "My image of him was always with a cigarette, and I think I associated smoking with being the man of the family. It was a grown-up thing to do."

Within several years, smoking became such an ingrained habit for Art that it blended into his self-image. "I think being a smoker has become a fabric in my personality. It is part of my body image to have a cigarette in hand."

Art has been smoking for almost thirty years now. That's almost 11,000 packs (some 220,000 cigarettes) at a cost of $15,000 to $20,000.

Art says he's tried to quit on and off ever since college; he's been successful from a week to eight months. At the time of this interview, he had not smoked for about six months, trying again to quit for life. The past two weeks, though, he's had an occasional cigarette, which has led up to two or three smokes a week. This is his typical pattern after he's tried to quit. "I know

I have to take a stand with myself, rediscover the reasons why I quit, or I'll be smoking again."

What exactly were those reasons? "I had been smoking a lot, sometimes feeling lousy with that oversmoked feeling at the end of the day—sort of achy, nauseated, and drained of energy by the end of the day—and my six-year-old daughter suddenly broke down crying one night because her friend had told her I was going to die from smoking. That made me quit."

Art says the worst part of quitting is breaking the psychological habit, including the ritual involved in using his hands, and its pleasurable flavor. After several months of abstaining from cigarettes, he starts thinking about those pleasures again until he finally smokes; then he smokes again after about every tenth thought. Soon he's back to his old habit.

Both his college-age sons have always been disgusted by and disdainful of his habit and "I agree with them." He has absolutely no doubt that cigarettes are hazardous to his health. "But I think that kids, like me, will be inclined to start smoking because it is a convenient way to fulfill certain needs"; these may be the need to look or act older, to feel calmed down by smoking or jacked up by nicotine, to rebel against parents and teachers, to share something forbidden with friends.

When asked what he'd say to kids today, with the wisdom of hindsight: "Once you start, it's very unlikely anyone like a parent or teacher can get you to stop. Yet I *know* that anyone who starts smoking will regret it for the rest of his or her life as he or she struggles with the habit. *You won't be able to do anything* about it later on as an adult because it's become so ingrained in you to smoke. But knowing that takes amazing foresight, which most kids don't have by their very nature. *But I guarantee they are going to regret they ever did such a stupid thing as start smoking.*"

—m—

Art should know. Six months after the interview, he was smoking yet again after trying to quit dozens of times over the years.

8

TEENS AND TOBACCO:
AN OVERVIEW

Every day 1,200 Americans die from smoking,[1] while 3,000 teenagers become confirmed smokers.[2] Half the teens who start smoking this year and smoke a lifetime can expect to die in their early sixties, fifteen years before their nonsmoking spouses and old friends from high school do.[3]

"Cigarettes kill more Americans than AIDS, alcohol, car accidents, murders, suicides, drugs and fires combined," states the 1994 Institute of Medicine report *Growing Up Tobacco Free: Preventing Nicotine Addiction in Children and Youths.*[4] We now know, it continues, that smoking is our nation's leading cause of preventable death and "the main cause of 87 percent of deaths from lung cancer, 30 percent of all cancer deaths, 82 percent of deaths from pulmonary disease, and 21 percent of deaths from chronic heart disease."[5]

Smoking-related illnesses, including diseases from passive smoking, account for almost 25 percent of all deaths among Americans[6] and claim about 30 percent of thirty-five- to sixty-nine-year-olds throughout the developed world.[7]

Every day 4,700 American adults stop buying cigarettes because they either die or quit the habit.[8] And every day tobacco companies shell out almost $13 million ($5 billion a year) for advertising to attract "replacement" smokers.[9] They largely court teenagers, who get hooked at almost the same rate as adults stopping. Why teenagers? Because tobacco companies know teens are far more likely to start smoking than any other

9

DEATHS FROM PREVENTABLE CAUSES IN THE UNITED STATES

Causes of Death
Tobacco vs. Other

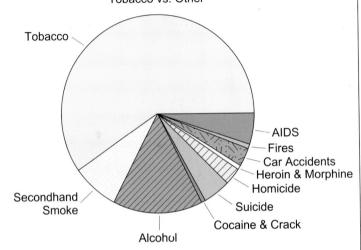

Tobacco

AIDS
Fires
Car Accidents
Heroin & Morphine
Homicide

Secondhand Smoke

Suicide

Cocaine & Crack

Alcohol

Annual Number of Deaths:

Tobacco .... 418,690[1]
Secondhand Smoke .... 53,000[2]
Alcohol (incl. drunk driving) .... 105,000[1]
Cocaine & Crack .... 3,300[3]
Heroin & Morphine .... 2,400[3]
Car Accidents .... 25,000[4]
Homicide .... 22,000[3]
Suicide .... 31,000[3]
Fires .... 4,000[4]
AIDS .... 33,745[1]

[1] U.S. Centers For Disease Control and Prevention
[2] U.S. Environmental Protection Agency
    Environmental Tobacco Smoke Compendium
[3] National Center For Health Statistics
[4] National Safety Council

Source: SmokeFree Educational Services, Inc., April 1995.

age group. In fact, the average U.S. smoker starts at age fourteen and a half.[10]

So it is kids and teens who feed this epidemic of smoking. "The facts are simple: one out of three adolescents in the United States is using tobacco by age 18, adolescent users become adult users, and few people begin to use tobacco after age 18," said Secretary of Health and Human Services Donna Shalala in the 1994 Surgeon General's Report *Preventing Tobacco Use Among Young People.*[11]

Kids are vulnerable to smoking because their transition to adulthood is fraught with stress, insecurity, and the need to be accepted by peers. If kids see smokers who they think are cool or look grown-up, they may strive for that image, too.

And to promote that image, tobacco companies bombard teens with a blitz of glossy, glitzy ads and promotions in stores, magazines, and buses, on roadside billboards, even on clothes and duffel bags at school. Teens are the "new recruits in the continuing epidemic of disease, disability and death attributable to tobacco use," says Donna Shalala.[12]

One outcome of this media blitz is that teens come to think of smoking as much more common than it really is. Teens may also wish they could be as smooth as Joe Camel or as sleek as Virginia Slim. Good advertising makes us want to be like the models in the ads. We think that maybe if we used the product, we'd be a little more like them, and so are willing to give it a try.

Or kids may smoke a few cigarettes as an experiment. They try a few smokes to fit in, to be sociable, to lose or keep off weight, to relax, or to rebel. A couple of Marlboros or Camels are forbidden enough to be exciting but don't seem too risky.

But unlike driving too fast or trying a dangerous sport, fooling around with cigarettes means inhaling a dose of nicotine, and scientists have shown that nicotine is at least as addictive as heroin and cocaine.[13] Once our body gets used to having nicotine, we crave it again and again simply to feel "right."

And so about a million kids start smoking *every year*. And

although they don't mean to get addicted, most can't help it if they start smoking enough that their bodies get used to nicotine. Smoking becomes not a choice, like working out, or a benign habit, like eating chocolate, but an addiction. Only one in ten who try kicking the addiction later on ever succeed.[14]

Even more alarming than the addictive nature of this easy-to-get and heavily promoted product is that today's kids, unlike older smokers, know full well the hazards of smoking. When many of today's smoking adults—twenty-four million men and twenty-two million women, a full quarter of the American adult population—started smoking, much of the scientific data linking smoking to fatal diseases had not yet emerged.[15]

So six million teenagers and 100,000 children (under age thirteen) smoke despite the knowledge that smoking is addictive and leads to a host of horrible diseases.[16] Yet youth smoking, which remained fairly steady in the 1980s, has been climbing in the 1990s.[17] Adult smoking, on the other hand, dropped steadily from the 1960s to 1990—from 40 percent to 26 percent[18]—and has remained fairly constant since then. Almost one-third of kids graduate from high school with more than a diploma—with a hard-to-quit, health-threatening habit.[19] That's very discouraging for public health officials who had hoped that a well-informed public would continue to quit smoking.

WORLDWIDE SMOKING

Worldwide, the picture is even grimmer. Smoking kills three million people each year around the globe, one person every ten seconds.[20] While most developed countries have steady or falling smoking rates, rates in developing countries—many already high—are rising 2 to 3 percent a year.[21] China alone has experienced annual 7 percent increases for a decade.[22] Currently 300 million Chinese adults smoke (61 percent of adult males, 7 percent of adult females)—there are more smokers in China than there are people in the entire United States![23] In Latin America and East Asia, one out of every two men smokes.

Dr. Alan Lopez of the World Health Organization estimates that of the 1.2 billion smokers alive today in developing countries, "about 200 million will be killed by tobacco, half in middle age."[24] Fueled by such vast numbers of present and future smokers, the worldwide death toll from smoking is expected to hit 10 million annually in twenty to thirty years.[25] Warns Dr. Lopez, "We are expecting a tidal wave of mortality."[26]

WHY? WHY? WHY?

Why do kids start smoking when they know cigarettes are addictive and deadly? Why can't they resist the social pressure to "just try" a butt? How do tobacco companies lure them into replacing the 4,700 customers who die or quit every day? Why do cigarettes remain one of the only—perhaps the only—legal addictive products, almost free from regulation, when scientific evidence has proven their very serious dangers?

To what extent should the rights of nonsmokers be protected against the health threat of smokers? How much in health care costs and lost productivity from smoking should society be willing to bear?

We'll be exploring these perplexing questions. First we'll see how teens and Americans in general got into this smoking mess in the first place (chapter 2). Then we'll see why kids say they smoke (chapter 3) and how tobacco companies spend billions trying to appeal to teenagers (chapter 4).

Next, we'll look at the health (chapter 5) and financial costs of smoking (chapter 6). We'll see how society is slowly changing its view of smoking from being "cool" to being a public health hazard (chapter 7). Then we'll explore how more and more people are suing tobacco companies over their ill health and blaming tobacco companies for ruthlessly targeting children and teenagers (chapter 8).

And finally we'll look at how this nation might resolve its teen epidemic of smoking and how teenagers and children can resist the enormous pressures to smoke.

13

2

HOW DID WE BECOME A
NATION OF TEEN SMOKERS?

We live in a country where about one-quarter of adults and up to 30 percent of teens finishing high school smoke cigarettes.[1]

How did we get to a time and place where more than one out of four of us smoke despite smoking's hazards to our health? Over the centuries, has tobacco been a blessing or a curse? A pleasure or a poison? An asset or an affliction? How has this robust—but unspectacular—plant come to play such a major role in world commerce, social history, and human health? How did smoking become such a common habit?

This chapter will trace tobacco's role and use through the ages to help us better understand how and why so many of us smoke cigarettes.

TOBACCO AND NATIVE AMERICANS

Tobacco (genus *Nicotiana*) belongs to the nightshade family of plants, which includes such diverse plants as potatoes, sweet peppers, petunias, and deadly nightshade. The species usually raised for cigarettes and cigars is *Nicotiana tabacum*. These plants may grow to be 4 to 6 feet high and bear huge rough and sticky leaves (8 to 14 inches wide and up to 20 inches long) that fan out from thick, strong stems topped with yellow or pink flowers.

Most experts believe that tobacco is native (grows naturally or wild) to the New World, what today is North and South America, including the United States. For centuries—from at least pre-Columbian times—these plants (*Nicotiana tabacum*) have flourished and have been cultivated in parts of South

A HURON LEGEND

A legend among the Huron Indians tells of a time when the world was barren. No plants could grow; people were dying as famine spread across the land. The Great Spirit sent a messenger—a girl—to save his people. Wherever the girl touched the ground with her right hand, potatoes appeared; wherever she placed her left hand, tall stalks of corn sprang up. The land became lush with food; people ate and regained their strength. The messenger sat down to rest. When she got up, yet another kind of plant was growing on her resting spot: a tobacco plant.

Some people say the legend shows how tobacco was a gift just like the potatoes and corn; others say that tobacco, delivered by the seat of the messenger, was a sign (or maybe a curse) from the Great Spirit that the gifts of food had their price.

America, the Caribbean islands, and Central America. A more bitter variety (*N. rustica*) grew in Mexico and the eastern parts of North America. Still other small-leaved species grew west of the Andes and the Rocky Mountains.

For hundreds of years before the first European explorers set foot in the New World, native peoples smoked, chewed, and snuffed tobacco. The Caribs of the West Indies breathed or snuffed a tobacco mixture through a hollow Y-shaped tube called a "taboca" or "tobago," from which the word *tobacco* was probably derived.[2] Natives of an island off Venezuela chewed tobacco "like cattle to such an extent that they could scarcely talk."[3] The Mayans smoked, as did North American tribes who had access to only a bitter variety (*N. rustica*) and so smoked long pipes (war pipes, peace pipes, pleasure pipes, or calumets) to temper the harsh flavor of those leaves.

For some, tobacco was considered a medicine to ease childbirth pain, heal wounds, ward off hunger, or alleviate thirst (because it stimulates salivation). Many tribes viewed tobacco as sacred and included it in wedding, birth, death, and war rituals.

Mayan priests believed its rising smoke carried messages to their gods. Others enjoyed tobacco for its smell. At different times, it also has been used as money or barter, as a measure of time (how long it took to smoke a pipe), and even as a way to induce hallucinations (when smoked and eaten in huge quantities).

But early accounts about tobacco also report that Native Americans smoked for its everyday pleasure. By the time the Europeans came to North America, the tobacco plant was so widespread in the New World, and smoking, chewing, and snuffing so common, that "not one native culture in temperate and tropical North, Central and South America was found to lack some form of tobacco usage."[4]

It was only a matter of time before the Europeans, after crossing the Atlantic, would also be lured by the appeal and pleasures of tobacco and smoking.

TOBACCO AND THE EXPLORERS

When Christopher Columbus and his Spanish crew (many of whom were just teenagers) arrived in the New World in 1492, they were showered with welcoming gifts from the natives. They relished the gifts of fruit and valued the wooden spears and other artifacts they received but threw out the dried and unfamiliar sweet-smelling leaves offered to them, thinking them worthless.

Some weeks later, however, the crew discovered a use for the leaves. Two of the crewmen, returning from a short scouting trip, reported having seen some Indians wrap the strange dried leaves "in the manner of a musket formed of paper,"[5] light one end, and breathe in smoke from the other. One of the two scouts, Rodrigo de Jerez, imitated what he had seen and became perhaps the first European tobacco smoker. When he later took his new habit home to Spain, priests there jailed him and denounced the smoke escaping from de Jerez's mouth as a sign of the devil. By the time de Jerez was released from prison

16

a few years later, however, the tide had turned: many Europeans had taken up smoking.

In most of the New World, European adventurers (many young men still in their teens) in both South and North America encountered tobacco and brought it back home to Spain, Portugal, France, England, and Holland. Along with leaves, seeds, and tools for using the tobacco, many of these adventurers also brought home a well-established tobacco habit. And while traveling home, these early entrepreneurs left tobacco seeds in far-flung places—the Philippines, India, Polynesia—and maintained tobacco fields along the sea routes to ensure themselves a supply of tobacco on future voyages. It was these sailors—first explorers and later merchants—crisscrossing the Atlantic or rounding the Horn of Africa, bound for the East, who were most responsible for the rapid spread of tobacco throughout Europe, Asia, and Africa.

TOBACCO AND THE EUROPEANS

In Europe, tobacco quickly caught on. It was soon considered a holy herb, even a wonder drug, with marvelous curative powers, good for "a remedy for female problems, a snakebite antidote, lung strengthener, ulcer remedy, cure for the plague, and potent aphrodisiac."[6] Jean Nicot de Villemain (after whom the words *nicotine* and the plant genus *Nicotiana* were named), the French

---

SIR WALTER RALEIGH'S SOGGY SMOKE

Legend has it that Sir Walter Raleigh (1551–1618) appeared at the court of England's Queen Elizabeth I puffing on a pipe. A servant believed Raleigh to be on fire and immediately doused him with beer to put it out. That soggy experience did not keep Raleigh from his beloved pipe tobacco. He popularized smoking both at court (the queen herself is said to have tried a pipe) and among the masses.

---

ambassador to Portugal, boasted widely of tobacco's so-called medicinal value and reportedly sent the French court its first snuff in the mid-sixteenth century. By the late 1500s the European appetite for tobacco was so great that small tobacco fields throughout the world were expanded into plantations to supply the ever-increasing demand.

Yet tobacco also had its critics, particularly clergymen (men of the church) and doctors. Spanish priests condemned smoking as a deal made with the devil. Some doctors, contrary to those who believed tobacco to be a cure-all, claimed that smoke filled the brain and blunted the senses. Others warned of sterility and birth defects. One English doctor wrote: "Tobacco causes vomit and is an enemy of the stomach."[7]

Some government leaders, believing tobacco to be evil, also tried to curb tobacco use. One Russian czar ordered that nostrils of snuffers be split so they couldn't indulge their habit; another czar ordered smokers whipped for their first offense, killed for a second. A Chinese emperor had tobacco importers beheaded, while a Turkish sultan executed as many as eighteen smokers a day![8]

Instead of abusing smokers or snuffers, some rulers tried to discourage tobacco use in other ways. King James I of England was an ardent tobacco opponent; in 1604 he denounced smoking as "loathsome," "hateful," and "dangerous to the lungs."[9] To control his countrymen's appetite for tobacco, James I limited tobacco imports. The resulting reduced supply simply fanned demand and pushed prices higher. At one point, a pound of tobacco was worth more than a pound of silver! James responded by boosting his tobacco tax 4,000 percent, assuming the huge duty would further curb imports.[10] This tactic also backfired. Smugglers grew rich, farmers grew tobacco . . . and more people than ever smoked.

James I eventually admitted defeat in his crusade against the "precious stink"[11] and turned England's tobacco cravings to his advantage: the government took control of importing and

18

selling tobacco, with revenues going into the national treasury. France, Italy, Russia, and Prussia soon followed suit. The governments grew richer on tobacco while the consciences of those who opposed tobacco use on moral or medical grounds were eased by the high taxes—today we refer to such taxes as "sin taxes."

TOBACCO, AMERICAN COLONISTS, AND EARLY AMERICANS

By 1620 tobacco was a booming commercial crop in the American colonies; by the end of the century an acre of tobacco was worth four times an acre of corn. Huge tobacco plantations, manned by thousands of slaves, dotted the Eastern Seaboard, especially in the Chesapeake tidewater region of Virginia and Maryland. By 1698 Virginia and Maryland together were exporting more than twenty-three million pounds of tobacco a year to Europe.[12]

Although colonial Americans used tobacco themselves, almost the entire tobacco crop was exported at that time. Pipes and snuff grew increasingly popular in the 1700s, mimicking habits abroad, and were viewed as a "creature comfort." To keep up the morale of his Revolutionary troops, George Washington, commander in chief of the armies and himself a successful to-bacco planter, begged for aid for his soldiers: "I say, if you can't send money, send tobacco."[13]

Just as tobacco use kept climbing elsewhere in the world, it did in the young United States. By the 1790s chewing tobacco became more stylish than the pipes and snuff of colonial times. Tobacco chewing was regarded as down-to-earth, a habit for "real men," both urban and rural. Chaw was practical and portable; no pipe, flame, or snuffbox was needed—just a place to spit!

Congressmen, particularly during Andrew Jackson's presi-dency (1829–1837), chewed tobacco as a way of linking them-selves with the common folk they represented. The British novelist Charles Dickens, on a U.S. tour, was appalled by this nation's filthy habit:

> Washington may be called the headquarters of tobacco-tinctured saliva. In all the public places of America, this filthy custom is recognized. In the courts of law, the judge has his spittoon, the crier his, the witness his, and the prisoner his.[14]

By 1860 America's tobacco appetite equaled the amount shipped abroad. Cigars grew in popularity, and by 1870 Americans (mostly males) smoked 1.2 billion cigars and used another 100 million pounds of tobacco in pipes, chewing tobacco, or snuff.[15] That's 60 cigars and 5 pounds of other tobacco used for every American male (from infants on up!) that year. Ten years later the figures had more than doubled: 2.75 billion cigars and 200 million pounds of pipe and chewing tobacco plus snuff were consumed in 1880.[16]

The use of tobacco continued to climb, fueled by a new, cheap smoke . . . the cigarette.

CIGARETTES

Native Americans smoked cigars (rolled tobacco leaves cemented with spit) and also made cigarettes ("small cigars") from tobacco scraps and waste. These early cigarettes caught on, according to one historian, with "lower-class people, members of the lesser breeds, and inferior individuals—which translated into children, the poor, and women."[17]

European cigarettes had a similar history. In the 1500s poor people often sifted through garbage to salvage cigar butts, partially burned pipe tobacco, and snuff dust. They mixed these tidbits together, rolled them in scrap paper, and puffed away— an inspired recycling effort that resulted in cheap (or free) smokes. A lower-class pleasure in Paris and London, cigarette smoking was later adopted by bohemians (artists, writers, revolutionaries) in many European cities.

During the Crimean War (1853–1856; a conflict in which Britain and France joined Turkey in its fight against Russia), however, the cigarette habit spread across classes and nations. Soldiers (again, many were teenagers) traded tobacco and picked up the habit, in an attempt to escape from the anxiety and boredom of war. As in future wars, tobacco use rose when soldiers brought their new habit home after the war.

CIGARETTES IN THE UNITED STATES

In the United States, it was the Civil War that spread the cigarette habit. Many soldiers took up smoking as a cheap, convenient way of consuming tobacco. After the war, soldiers introduced friends to cigarettes. Cigars were still the gentleman's smoke, but more and more ordinary people began smoking cigarettes as a low-cost alternative.

By the 1880s high-speed machines for mass-producing cigarettes were vastly increasing cigarette production. In 1890 per capita (how much per person, including children, in the nation) consumption rose to 35 cigarettes each. In 1910 the figure was 85, and by 1930 it had skyrocketed to almost 1,000![18]

War was to spread cigarettes once again even deeper into American culture. During World War I (1914–1918), an army doctor reported that the cigarette "is an indispensable comfort to the men."[19] General John J. Pershing, head of the U.S. Army in Europe, cabled home: "Tobacco is as indispensable as the daily ration; we must have thousands of tons of it without delay."[20] At another time, Pershing said, "You ask me what we need to win this war. I answer tobacco as much as bullets."[21] During these times, cigarettes "came to be identified with all the positive values—quiet dignity, courage, and dedication above all."[22]

World War II (1939–1945) had much the same effect on spreading the smoking habit. Most soldiers, sailors, and pilots (many of whom were in their teens) smoked with gusto, and Americans at home followed suit. Cigarettes were again deemed essential to the morale of the troops and were included in field

21

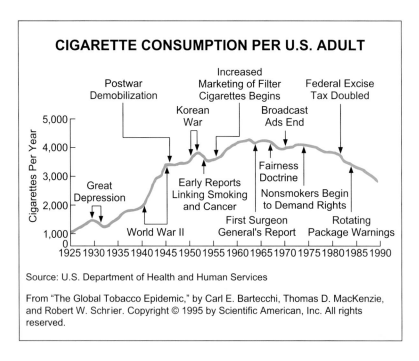

CIGARETTE CONSUMPTION PER U.S. ADULT

Source: U.S. Department of Health and Human Services

From "The Global Tobacco Epidemic," by Carl E. Bartecchi, Thomas D. MacKenzie, and Robert W. Schrier. Copyright © 1995 by Scientific American, Inc. All rights reserved.

rations (along with dehydrated soup, lemonade mix, and Spam). President Franklin D. Roosevelt classified tobacco as an essential crop and required draft boards to give deferments to tobacco farmers to ensure maximum production. By the end of the war, cigarette sales were higher than ever before. Billboards, radios, movies, magazines, and newspapers carried engaging cigarette ads with catchy jingles. By 1947 per capita cigarette consumption in the United States was 128 packs of cigarettes smoked for every man, woman, and child![23] Three out of every four men smoked cigarettes; half that number of women smoked; teenagers smoked. America was hooked.

CIGARETTES AND KIDS: PROTECTING AMERICA'S YOUTH

As cigarettes grew more popular, opponents grew more vocal. The early anti-tobacco movement, led by educators and reformers, rallied to protect the nation's youth (specifically boys) from

22

the evils of smoking. By 1890 twenty-six states had passed laws prohibiting the sale of cigarettes to minors. Few, however, paid much attention to the laws, which were difficult to enforce.

But one reformer, Lucy Page Gaston, believed that smoking led to drink, disease, crime, and death; she founded the Chicago Anti-Cigarette League in 1899. Among other activities, the league hired officers to arrest anyone younger than eighteen seen smoking in public and tried to prohibit the sale of cigarettes as the only sure way to keep cigarettes away from youth.

Others also spoke out about the destructive influence of cigarettes on youth, saying that smoking lowered intelligence, school performance, and lung capacity and promoted insomnia, high blood pressure, and bronchial problems. Moral arguments were also offered. The president of the New York City Board of Education said that "cigarette fiends" in public schools stole money for smokes, and concluded that the "cigarette habit is more devastating to the health and morals of young men than any habit or vice that can be named."[24] Cigarettes were also blamed for rising juvenile crime rates.

The anti-cigarette efforts worked, but only briefly. By 1909 fifteen states banned cigarette sales completely, yet cigarette use kept climbing. The laws were eventually repealed. To make cigarettes even more attractive, tobacco companies launched an aggressive advertising campaign showing cigarettes as a symbol of youth and beauty. Soon middle-class women and teenagers were taking up the habit as never before.

By 1952, 800,000 teenagers were picking up the habit every year.[25] At the same time, however, researchers were slowly but surely linking cigarette smoking with lung cancer, heart disease, and other serious health problems.

SMOKING, HEALTH, AND TODAY'S SMOKING PATTERNS

By the early 1960s researchers had substantial evidence that cigarette smoking was linked to lung cancer and an overall higher death rate. One study of men between the ages of forty-five and sixty-four, for example, found that death rates of smokers were twice as high as those of nonsmokers, while death rates from lung cancer among smokers were ten times higher![26] These rates were confirmed by a study of more than one million American adults conducted in the 1960s: 1,385 smokers died during the study, compared to 662 nonsmokers. Of the smokers, 110 had died from lung cancer, compared with only 12 deaths among nonsmokers. More than twice as many smokers (654) died of coronary heart disease than did nonsmokers (304).[27] Differences in numbers of deaths due to emphysema and various cancers (mouth, pharynx, larynx, esophagus, pancreas, and bladder) were also striking.

In 1961 representatives from major American health organizations urged President John F. Kennedy to do something about the tobacco problem. He responded by forming the Surgeon General's Advisory Committee on Smoking and Health. In 1964 the committee published its report, *Smoking and Health*. The conclusions were sobering: cigarette smoking is a major cause of lung cancer; smokers are nine or ten times more likely to get lung cancer than are nonsmokers; the more a person smokes, the greater are his chances of contracting lung cancer; smoking also contributes to heart disease, bronchitis, and emphysema.

At first Americans took the report to heart. Cigarette sales declined 20 percent within two months.[28] But habit and heavy advertising led to a rebound—cigarette sales in 1965 were 562 billion, the highest ever.[29]

In 1966 cigarette packages were required by law to carry a health-hazard warning. By 1971 cigarette advertising was banned from television and radio.

Gradually Americans began to heed the health warnings and give up cigarettes. Smokers declined from 40 percent of the adult population in 1965 to almost 26 percent in 1991, and the percentage has held steady since then.[30]

24

Today about 46 million—about one-quarter—of American adults smoke cigarettes; 44 million have kicked the habit.[31] In fact, among American males today, there are more former smokers than current smokers. Even current smokers have gotten the message: four out of every five adult smokers say they would like to quit.[32] Unfortunately, teens have not followed the same trend.

SMOKING AND TEENS

Historically, male teens have come of age as adults much earlier than they do today. As adult smoking caught on, so did teen smoking. By age sixteen or seventeen, teen boys were considered adult, old enough to marry and fight in wars. The trends we've discussed historically have included these older teens.

In the twentieth century, however, teens have been more separate from adults, not coming of age until their late teens or even early twenties. In the late 1960s and early 1970s the baby boomers (the generation born after World War II), now teenagers, began to smoke. In fact, they smoked more cigarettes per day than did their parents.[33] In 1976 about 38 percent of high-school seniors reported regular smoking (within the past thirty days), and approximately 28 percent were daily smokers. Most were light smokers (half a pack per day or less); only 3 percent smoked more than a pack per day.[34]

As medical evidence against cigarettes mounted, the rate of youth smoking dropped until 1980, when it leveled off. In 1980 about 30 percent of high-school seniors were regular smokers and 21 percent were daily smokers.[35]

Although these figures remained steady for more than a decade, teen smoking has been climbing recently. For example, the number of eighth graders who smoke at least once a month jumped 30 percent between 1991 and 1994.[36] In 1994 one out of every five eighth graders and one out of every three twelfth graders smoked cigarettes.[37]

Next we'll examine why so many teens smoke.

25

Alex

Alex is a high-school senior in upstate New York. He started smoking at fourteen, hanging around with friends.

"We were sitting around, and a few guys were smoking. A friend asked me to hold his cigarette, and I took a drag. I felt kind of dizzy and sick to my stomach, but I had two more that day. Then I kept doing it and doing it, and soon it became a habit. Now I smoke a pack of Marlboros a day."

Alex admits he's not a very good student; he spends a lot of his time either hanging out with friends, shooting hoops, or listening to country music. He says almost all his friends smoke.

"It becomes an addiction very quickly. It's really easy to get addicted and really hard to quit. I haven't tried to quit, but I can't go a day without a cigarette; if I can't get a smoke, I'm not a very nice person to be around."

Alex says that his habit isn't so much psychological as physical. "It's definitely my body. If I don't have a cigarette first thing in the morning, I get kind of shaky and get in a really bad mood."

Alex started smoking even though he says he knew cigarettes were bad for him: "Yeah, I've been through all the health courses in school and I knew that stuff, but I didn't really listen. It's such a long time down the road that I'd experience any ill effects I didn't really think about it at the moment. Besides, my grandmother's been smoking for years—she's sixty-nine—and my stepgrandfather has been smoking since he was nine and his ninetieth birthday is tomorrow. So I don't think I have anything to worry about. They can't prove that all that stuff [illness] is from cigarettes. Some people die of natural causes even if they smoke, and I just hope I'll be one of those people."

Why does he smoke? "It calms me down when I'm in a really bad mood. It gives me time to think things through. Once in a while it gives me a little head rush, too." He also likes the fact that he's lost weight and seems in better shape since he's started smoking, "although I can't run as far as I used to—I get out of breath—but I don't run very often."

Alex says that although he's never tried to quit ("I don't think about it"), his mom gets on his case from time to time. "And a couple of girlfriends have ragged on me, but that hasn't been important."

Even though Alex enjoys his cigarettes, he'd tell younger kids to stay away. "It's not a good habit, it's really expensive and not a good habit to start, but once I started, I haven't been able to stop. I don't mind it personally, but I don't advocate smoking for younger kids. It's a really expensive habit, and kids who don't have money would spend what they have on cigarettes."

—m—

Alex seems to be one of those kids who started smoking because his friends smoked. Although he's learned that cigarettes are bad for him, he uses the case of his stepgrandfather to justify to himself that they're not bad for everyone. Since harm from cigarettes is so far down the road for him, he doesn't think now about the harm he might be doing to himself. Like many teens, he just thinks about today and the immediate gratification of enjoying a cigarette.

In giving advice to younger kids, he thinks only of the cost of cigarettes; he seems to put the potentially devastating effects of cigarettes on his future health completely out of his mind.

Like many teens, Alex believes he is invulnerable and will remain unharmed by a potentially very dangerous behavior even though he has been taught otherwise.

3

WHY TEENS SMOKE

Every day some 3,000 American kids become regular smokers.[1] That's one million kids a year, year after year. By age thirteen, some 56 percent of American children have tried smoking; 9 percent are already regular smokers.[2] By seventeen, a whopping 77 percent of American teens have tried smoking; one-quarter of the entire teen population smokes frequently.[3]

Despite health classes on the horrors of smoking, complete with photos of diseased lungs, kids still smoke. Why? What is the appeal of taking a drag on that first cigarette? What makes one teen more likely to try smoking than another? And why do so many end up with a pack-a-day habit?

THE POWER OF PEERS AND SIBLINGS

More than any other age group, teens are most influenced by other kids close in age or slightly older, including siblings. Four out of five teenagers smoke their first cigarettes with friends, siblings, or acquaintances; only 11 percent of teens first try smoking alone.[4] A twelve- to fourteen-year-old is four times more likely to smoke if he or she has a best friend who smokes[5]—when best friends smoke, teens are thirteen times more likely to have smoked within the past month than those whose best friends do not smoke.[6]

Having an older sister or brother who smokes also exerts a strong influence because younger siblings often look up to their older siblings and want to emulate them.

Sometimes kids feel pressured by peers to smoke. In describing their first experiences with cigarettes, more than one-third of teens report being encouraged by friends or even teased and taunted into smoking.[7]

Other times, friends provide company and support for one another and satisfy one another's curiosity about cigarettes. In fact, two-thirds of teen smokers report that curiosity was the primary reason behind their first few cigarettes.[8]

OTHER ROLE MODELS: PARENTS AND SIBLINGS

Researchers aren't sure if having a parent who smokes affects whether or not a teen will smoke. Of fifteen studies on parental smoking, seven showed that having a parent who smoked predicted that a child would smoke; two found it was a factor only with daughters; and six showed parental smoking had no effect.[9]

About 45 percent of eighth graders report that their parents' opposition to smoking is a major reason why they don't smoke; but by twelfth grade only 27 percent say that parents make a difference.[10] Although strict parental attitudes about smoking can prevent some kids from smoking, they can also backfire. Ten- to twelve-year-olds who think their parents are too strict, for example, were found in one study to be *more* likely to start smoking.

THE NEED FOR SOCIAL ACCEPTANCE

Teens want to fit in with peer groups they admire—the "cool" kids—and many will do what "cool" kids do. Allison, a teen from suburban Connecticut, describes how she began to smoke: "I was fourteen, at summer sleep-away camp, with all these girls my age who were from New York City. They all smoked and I thought they looked so cool."[11]

Kids are particularly vulnerable at parties. According to twenty teens from the Baltimore area, 75 to 90 percent of kids they know smoke at parties. As one high-school senior told a *U.S. News & World Report* journalist, "It makes you look like you belong."[12] A tenth-grade girl agreed: "For people who are insecure, it's something they have in common with other people."[13]

"EVERYONE'S DOING IT," KIDS THINK, BUT IT'S NOT TRUE

Cigarette ads try to make us think that smoking is a widespread and completely acceptable thing to do. When asked what an ad of Joe's Place conveyed—with camels smoking and dancing amid potted palms and pool tables—one high-school freshman replied, "Join the party! Everybody's doing it!"[14] Teens who see their friends with cigarettes after school or at parties tend to conclude that smoking is much more common among their peers than it really is. Many come to think that smoking is normal behavior for teens, a behavior to be emulated in order to be one of the crowd.

Teens—even nonsmokers—routinely overestimate how many people smoke. A Michigan study found, for example, that 79 percent of teens thought that more than half of all adults smoked cigarettes and 68 percent believed that more than half of all teens smoked. Both estimates are twice the real numbers.[15] Teens who smoke have even wilder misconceptions: teen smokers in one study estimated that 55 percent of all eighth and ninth graders smoked, when in fact fewer than 11 percent smoked.[16] When kids think so many others smoke, they are much more likely to smoke themselves.

TO REDUCE STRESS

Some teens report they smoke to reduce the stress in their lives. Puberty and adolescence are times of emotional, physical, and psychological upheaval. Preteens and teens feel anxiety about their bodies, feelings, and cultural roles, which are in a flux. They must cope with their emerging sexuality, independence, and personal values. It's not surprising, therefore, that smoking begins most frequently in grades six through nine and then levels off.

Kids smoke not only because of the anxieties and pressures of adolescence but also because of depression. Teens with a history of depression are more apt to become smokers, according to researchers. Since the nicotine in cigarettes boosts the levels of certain brain chemicals that are stimulating and can produce a mild "high," depressed teens may well use cigarettes as a way of relieving their despair. For some of these teens, smoking isn't help enough. High-school students who smoke heavily are eighteen times more likely than nonsmokers to attempt suicide; light smokers are five to six times more apt to try suicide.[17]

REBELLION AND THE QUEST FOR INDEPENDENCE

As teens reach out to their peer groups more and more for approval and acceptance, many rebel against society and its conventions. Smoking allows them to do both. Allison, the girl who began smoking at summer camp with her New York City bunkmates, relished smoking's dual role. Not only did she fit in with her "cool" new friends but she thumbed her nose at society: "Smoking was one of my first rebellious acts, you know?"[18]

Some teens will smoke in direct defiance of a parent's wishes. Megan, a fourteen-year-old from Delaware, had been lectured by her mother about the dangers of smoking. Megan said, "I knew she didn't want me to do it [smoke], so I did it."[19]

Although smoking is fraught with hazard, cigarettes have a certain allure that no amount of reasoning seems to overcome. It's as if the more adults in positions of authority (such as parents, physicians, scientists) denounce cigarettes, the more attractive they become to certain teenagers who tend to want to mildly defy authority. One teen from Baltimore declared, "A lot of people smoke to give the finger to the world."[20] Joe, a ninth grader, also from Baltimore, speculated,

31

"I think there's some people who want to be bad but without being a criminal."[21]

TO CONTROL WEIGHT

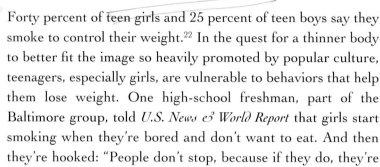

Forty percent of teen girls and 25 percent of teen boys say they smoke to control their weight.[22] In the quest for a thinner body to better fit the image so heavily promoted by popular culture, teenagers, especially girls, are vulnerable to behaviors that help them lose weight. One high-school freshman, part of the Baltimore group, told *U.S. News & World Report* that girls start smoking when they're bored and don't want to eat. And then they're hooked: "People don't stop, because if they do, they're afraid they'll gain weight."[23]

Cigarette ads shamelessly play upon girls' obsessions about weight control. A very thin model holding a Virginia Slims (itself long and thin) announces, for example, "If I ran the world, calories wouldn't count."

Smoking does in fact raise the body's basal metabolic rate slightly. Smokers burn a few more calories—from thirty-one to sixty-nine more during eight hours—than nonsmokers; that's the equivalent of about an apple or cookie a day, which can add up to a difference of about a pound a month.[24] People who smoke and then quit, in fact, usually gain five to ten pounds, partly because they eat instead of smoke, but also because their metabolism slows down a bit.

THE LURE OF RISKS AND SENSE OF INVULNERABILITY

Teenagers have always engaged in more high-risk behaviors than any other age group. These behaviors include drinking, doing drugs, driving too fast, and having unprotected sex. Teenagers typically feel strong, fearless, and invulnerable to accidents and illnesses, believing "it can't happen to me." That sense of invulnerability, coupled with a short-term perspective, leads many kids to act without clear foresight.

Other teens believe that a few cigarettes can't hurt, and since they don't feel addicted, they think they could quit at any time. Still others admit the long-term effects but choose to disregard them.

WHY ARE SOME TEENS MORE APT TO SMOKE THAN OTHERS?

Teens themselves view smoking as a way to relax, have fun, fit in with the "cooler" crowd, cope with boredom, stress, personal problems, and/or weight problems. Yet most kids—three out of four—don't smoke; they resist short-term pleasure and temptation for long-term safety and health. What makes some kids more likely to succumb to the short-term lure? Researchers have found that these traits put kids at higher risk for smoking:

- Low self-esteem; therefore, more susceptibility to peer pressure (can't refuse the offer of a cigarette)
- Low academic achievement (up to 70 percent of high-school dropouts smoke)[25]
- Few or no goals for the future
- Low socioeconomic status (perhaps because of more personal and financial stress, more dysfunctional or one-parent families, less parental supervision, more role models who smoke)

Interestingly, however, African-American teens don't follow these patterns. Their smoking rate has fallen steadily since 1976. While it once matched the rate of whites, now just 4 percent smoke daily, compared with 23 percent of white teens.[26] No one can explain this dramatic difference—"We want to bottle it, so we can sustain it for black teens and pass it along to white teens," says Michael Eriksen, director of the U.S. Centers for Disease Control and Prevention's Office on Smoking and Health.[27]

ADDICTION

We've seen why so many kids—from 47 to 90 percent[28]—experiment at least once with cigarettes. What too few realize, however, is that with every drag on a cigarette, the body becomes increasingly dependent and soon addicted to the nicotine (see chapter 5 for details on how nicotine affects the body).

"Nicotine dependency through cigarette smoking is not only the most common form of drug addiction but the one that causes more death and disease than all other addictions combined," according to the Surgeon General's Report.[29] While smoking a cigarette—or even a daily pack of cigarettes—may *seem* relatively harmless compared to a heroin, cocaine, or alcohol habit, nicotine is more addictive in many ways. Traits of addiction include using a substance more than intended; craving it and being unable to quit; feeling withdrawal symptoms (irritability, agitation, headaches) if deprived and taking the substance to relieve or avoid withdrawal; and using it despite knowing its harm.

There is no question that teens fit these descriptions for nicotine addiction or dependency. They consume sizable amounts of nicotine; they encounter withdrawal symptoms (irritability, restlessness, trouble concentrating, physical and psychological cravings for cigarettes) when they can't smoke; and they have difficulty quitting. Dependent teens typically report that they smoke for pleasure—and because they are addicted. Three-fourths of daily cigarette smokers (ages ten to twenty-two) report that one of the reasons they smoke is because it is hard to quit.[30]

While nicotine may not intoxicate the way that heroin, cocaine, alcohol, and marijuana do, Dr. Jack Henningfield and Dr. Neal Benowitz, experts on addiction, ranked it first in "dependence."[31] Dependence is determined by how hard it is to quit, how many people try to quit and can't, how desperately users feel the need for the substance, and how much people use it even though they know it's harmful. Nicotine ranked third for "withdrawal," after alcohol and heroin.

Allison, the teen from Connecticut, who began smoking four years ago, says, "I don't think I could quit right now. I don't want to have to go without a cigarette. I get so irritable if I can't have one when I want to."[32]

Cathy, a seventeen-year-old from Delaware, smoked for more than three years. She thought her social smoking was under control—until she tried to quit. "I realized I was addicted and I didn't want to be. I also realized many of the stronger people, the leaders, didn't smoke."[33]

Ironically, most teens who are addicted to tobacco really do want to quit but can't. It's too late; going without a cigarette has gotten too hard.

ACCESSIBILITY

Urged to smoke by friends, advertisements, and physiological need, teens can all too easily get cigarettes to satisfy their desire. Although it's illegal in all fifty states to sell cigarettes to people under the age of eighteen, the laws are rarely enforced. In 1989 an estimated 1.5 million of the nation's 2.6 million underage smokers bought their own cigarettes.[34] In four years of illegally buying cigarettes, Allison told *Consumer Reports*, "I can count on one hand the number of times I've been carded [by a sales-person]."[35] Study after study confirms that cigarettes are readily available—over the counter or from vending machines—to anyone of virtually any age. Being able to get cigarettes so easily merely increases the chances of teens becoming regular smokers.

THE STAGES OF SMOKING

We've seen why kids are attracted to trying cigarettes in the first place and how they get hooked on nicotine. Typically, this is how the habit of smoking develops, usually over a two- or three-year period:[36]

- **Preparatory stage:** A child learns about smoking and is influenced by advertising and adult, sibling, or peer role models. No cigarettes are smoked.
- **Trying stage:** The greater the availability of cigarettes, the number of friends who smoke, and the stronger the perception that smoking is an acceptable and common behavior, the greater the chances the person will progress to this stage. The first few cigarettes are smoked, usually with friends.
- **Experimental stage:** Having friends who smoke, being unable to refuse offers of cigarettes, being able to get cigarettes easily, and social situations where smoking is common all contribute to this stage. The teenager or preteen smokes irregularly but repeatedly (e.g., only at parties or only with a best friend).
- **Regular use:** By this stage, kids often feel that cigarettes help them in some way (e.g., to relieve stress or look grown-up). That belief, coupled with peers who smoke and the lack of smoking restrictions at home or in the community, contribute to regular (at least weekly) smoking in a variety of situations.
- **Addiction/dependent smoker:** The teenager has developed a physiological need for the nicotine in cigarettes and smokes often and regularly to satisfy that need. The teen is hooked, probably for decades.

—w—

We've explored the underlying causes of why teens first light up and how that progresses to a full smoking habit. These stages of smoking, however, are further glamorized, reinforced, and perpetuated by billion-dollar advertising campaigns and the glitzy worlds of music and movies. Next we'll look at how the media contribute to the fact that one out of four teenagers smokes cigarettes.

Mary Rose

Mary Rose, a junior in a high school in Kentucky tobacco country, lives with a smoking family. Two of three older sisters smoke, as does her father. "Sometimes he quits, but that's a joke. He just can't." Both her grandfather and great-grandfather on her dad's side died of smoking-related cancer. "And my dad's got no teeth and I don't want to end up like that. My sister, she's twenty-three, she's got teeth that are all brown, all that stuff on them, yech. She started smoking at thirteen or fourteen."

Her father owns land and pays others to raise tobacco on it. "A lot of people smoke around here. I think smoking's pretty nasty—it makes the halls in our school stink."

Nevertheless, Mary Rose started smoking on and off last year. "At parties, you feel pressured," she says. So she smokes occasionally but has never bought or smoked a whole pack. So far, she estimates she's probably smoked only about fifteen or twenty cigarettes. "Sometimes I get an urge and feel like maybe it's becoming a habit, but it's nothing major. My friends don't smoke all the time, so I don't feel any big thing."

It's been a month, she estimates, since she's had a cigarette because soccer season started a month ago. "Sometimes I get worried about feeling addicted. I think I was a little before soccer season, but then I got caught by my parents. Besides, I can't smoke during soccer—you feel different when you smoke and I gotta run three miles a day. I can't do that if I'm smoking."

Mary Rose says that cigarettes don't taste very good to her and don't actually appeal to her. "I don't like them, so I'm not worried about getting hooked." Then why does she ever smoke? "I don't know why I do it. Just being with my friends, I guess. When you're with the group you want to fit in, so you smoke. If I go with them, I'd want to smoke again. If my friends are smoking, I'll want to sometimes."

—๛—

Mary Rose says she thinks cigarettes could be addictive but she's not worried about that because she doesn't really like how they taste. Nevertheless, Mary Rose smokes occasionally and, without realizing it, she could easily become addicted to the nicotine. If more than forty million Americans have gotten hooked, why not Mary Rose? Unfortunately, all too many kids play around with cigarettes and, without ever meaning to, become addicted. They can't help it. Nicotine *is* addictive.

4

HOW CIGARETTE ADVERTISING SEEKS CONSUMERS AND SEDUCES TEENS

It's one thing to have a buddy offer you a smoke every once in a while or see your friends light up at a party. It's another to be confronted day after day by the most glitzy, glossy images that ad agencies can produce. Signs of cigarettes are everywhere: in two-page color spreads in best-selling magazines, on billboards lining well-traveled highways, at televised sporting events and music concerts, in eye-catching displays at convenience stores and gas stations, on shirts and caps worn by kids in all kinds of places. Even private homes are no sanctuary from the advertising blitz: bright, alluring fliers are often tucked into private mailboxes to promote a new brand or entice new customers from unsuspecting millions retrieving their mail.

What does this pervasive tobacco promotion do? It not only creates the perception that more people smoke than actually do, says former Surgeon General Joycelyn Elders in the 1994 Surgeon General's Report on teen smoking, but also "provides a conduit between actual self-image and ideal self-image—in other words, smoking is made to look cool."[1] Whether these influences actually *cause* smoking or not, they encourage "the uptake of smoking, initiating for many a dismal and relentless chain of events."[2]

Indeed, the images used to promote smoking try to make it look as cool and attractive as possible. They are designed to grab your attention and entice you to become a "wannabe." Consider a few of these images:

- Three young, fun-seeking, and hip African-Americans on ice skates dribble a basketball. "Alive with pleasure!" proclaims the ad for Newports.

- Joe Camel sports a T-shirt, jacket, and shades; a cigarette dangles casually, and oh so suavely, between his second and third fingers. The epitome of "cool," he invites you to browse through his Camel Cash catalog.

- Race-car driver Al Unser Jr. gives a thumbs-up signal as he peers out from under the visor of his Marlboro racing helmet, on the cover page of a special Indy Car advertising section in *Sports Illustrated.*

- As tennis star Steffi Graf powers a backhand, the words *Virginia Slims* bedeck the stadium wall behind her.

Just how do these images — Joe Camel, the Marlboro Man, and the sleek Virginia Slims models — help lure young teens into smoking?

A BASEBALL PLAYER FIGHTS BACK

The 1909 baseball card of Honus Wagner has become the most valuable baseball card in the world (it sold for $450,000 in 1991). At that time, baseball cards were used to promote cigarettes and served as "package stiffeners." But Wagner, an avid anti-smoker, tried to have all his cards destroyed, "furious that his image was being used to sell cigarettes to children."

—*In* Tobacco Biology and Politics, *by Stanton A. Glantz*

WHY THEY TARGET TEENAGERS

Every single day tobacco companies want 5,000 people to start smoking to replace the 3,500 Americans who quit smoking and 1,200 who die from smoking-related illnesses that day.[3] Five thousand people every day, two million each year. The tobacco companies know that almost everyone—89 percent of adults[4]—who smokes regularly started smoking as a teenager. The earlier a person starts smoking, the more years—and cigarettes—he or she is likely to smoke in a lifetime. Teens are perfect targets.

To attract new smokers—and to convince established smokers to switch brands—American tobacco companies spend billions of dollars just to advertise. In the past twenty years, while many adult smokers were quitting, tobacco companies quadrupled their outlays for advertising and promotion, from $1.2 billion in 1975 to $4.6 billion in 1991. That's $12.6 million a day, $8,750 per minute; or $18 annually for every adult and child in the United States.[5] Only automobile manufacturers spend more money on marketing campaigns.

WHAT CIGARETTE ADVERTISING TRIES TO DO

Print advertisements (in newspapers and magazines, on billboards and posters) give information about cigarettes, such as tar and nicotine content, filter features, or low cost, but even more important, they try to change attitudes about a product. The ads create an impression that a certain type of person—fun-loving, sophisticated, outdoorsy, independent—smokes a particular brand of cigarette. They try to attract young people to the "glamour" of smoking while creating the impression that smoking is very acceptable.

In general, the ads attempt to:

- influence nonsmokers so they might sometime experiment with cigarettes,
- show that smoking is a normal activity in certain contexts,
- offset and minimize the dangers of smoking,
- convince smokers that the benefits of smoking are well worth the risks, and
- get coupons, discounts, special displays, and catalogs to potential smokers.

MESSAGES THE ADS TRY TO CONVEY

The best advertising creates impressions and influences people without their being aware of that influence. Nevertheless, cigarette advertisements (and the promotions that complement the ads) are very specific in trying to get across certain messages. These are

• "Smoking is a way to be independent."
The Marlboro Man (or Cowboy), for example, is rugged, sexy, tough, and fiercely independent and does whatever he wants. One teen described the message of these ads as "When you're smoking you're unstoppable."[6] The Marlboro Man appeals to defiant adolescents trying to break away from childhood rules. That appeal has translated into sales: about 70 percent of all new smokers light up these "children's cigarettes."[7]

• "Smoking is a rite of passage to adulthood."
Teenagers want to think of themselves as grown-up and so are attracted to adult themes—adventure, independence again, sophistication, glamour, and sex. In fact, adolescents are drawn more to adult models than to young ones.

• "Successful, popular people smoke."
Consider Joe Camel and his crowd of partying friends, the close-knit Newport buddies frolicking outdoors, or the happy Benson & Hedges gang atop the Statue of Liberty. Such images give the impression that if you smoke, you will be like the models or characters pictured. As one boy put it, "People who buy the cigarettes think if they [models] can smoke and be pretty and thin and have fun, maybe I can, too."[8]

• "Tobacco use is relaxing in social situations."
Cigarettes seem to make you fit in, a major concern to many adolescents. Again, Joe Camel and his relaxed and happy friends are a familiar example.

42

> **MARLBORO MAN**
>
> "I have a particular reason for disapproving of smoking. My late brother, David Millar, died of emphysema complications caused by smoking. He was, ironically, the first Marlboro Man."
>
> —*The late Marlboro Man's sister in* Kids Say Don't Smoke

- "Tobacco use is the norm."

By placing smokers (or presumed smokers—none of the models are actually smoking, and only a handful hold cigarettes) in everyday situations, these ads create the impression that smoking is a common, acceptable thing to do. They picture activities or situations to which teens can relate, such as friends meeting after work, a Kool man settling down for a smoke, or a Merit couple celebrating a strike at the bowling alley. The sheer volume of cigarette advertising strengthens the notion that smoking is widespread.

- "Tobacco use is safe and healthful."

Ads picture healthy, active people, often engaged in wholesome outdoor activities: skiers swooping past a Kool sign on their way down a mountain trail, or the Marlboro Man gazing at the Montana landscape. Sometimes outdoor scenes are used instead of models to convey a "healthy" image: an Alpine ("mountain-fresh") ad showing a deep blue lake nestled between soaring, snow-covered peaks. Words such as *light, mild, clean, fresh, soft,* and *natural* promote this message as well.

THE MULTIMEDIA MARKETING OF CIGARETTES

Two decades ago, most advertising appeared in magazines and newspapers; these days, however, the focus has shifted to various kinds of promotional activities and items, including coupons that can be redeemed for logo-bearing paraphernalia. One reason the promotions are so popular now is that they don't have to carry the health warnings required in printed advertisements.

Nevertheless, tobacco companies use a wide range of tactics to attract new smokers, including teenagers.

Magazine and Newspaper Advertising

Cigarette ads in magazine and newspapers comprised only a small fraction—7 percent—of the money spent on advertising in 1991, down from 46 percent in 1980.[9] The cutback has been in adult magazines; magazines popular with young people still have lots of ads: *Sports Illustrated*, *TV Guide*, *People*, *Glamour*, *Mademoiselle*, *Elle*, *National Lampoon*, and *Rolling Stone* all carry cigarette ads, as do magazines for African-Americans such as *Jet*, *Essence*, and *Ebony*. As one high-school girl said, "They advertise a lot. Every magazine I have—there's an ad for Camels, Marlboros, Newports."[10]

Effect on Teens: With so many ads in magazines they read, teens are likely to get the erroneous impression that smoking is more popular than it really is. Also, the magazines that carry lots of cigarette ads (and therefore make lots of money from tobacco companies) tend not to run articles about the dangers of smoking. These trends contribute to the distorted view that smoking isn't all that bad.

Outdoor Advertising

Almost 10 percent of tobacco marketing dollars spent in 1991 went for outdoor advertising—roadside billboards and signs on buses, trains, and subways. As in the case of magazine ads, the billboards are in carefully chosen locations. Despite the industry's self-imposed regulations against such placement, billboards can often be found near places frequented by kids—schools, playgrounds, churches, and shopping centers.

Cigarette billboards in professional sports stadiums were particularly effective for the tobacco companies until the mid-1990s, when many were removed voluntarily or by local policy.

Not only did sports fans see the billboards while at the stadium, but millions of TV viewers saw them at home. According to the Surgeon General's Report, "Each 3-second exposure of a billboard in a ballpark [on TV] has a marketing impact similar to a 10-second TV commercial."[11]

Effect on Teens: Plastering ads on billboards, where teens unconsciously see them day in and day out over the course of years, reinforces the notion that cigarette smoking is common, normal behavior. Warning labels are completely dwarfed by pictures of happy, apparently healthy smokers.

Value-Added Promotions

The fastest-growing form of cigarette marketing (40 percent of the cigarette marketing pie spent in 1991)[12] is known as value-added promotions and coupons. These are cents-off coupons, buy-one-get-one-free offers, twenty-five-cigarette packs, and free items (lighters, key chains) attached to packs of cigarettes.

Effect on Teens: These promotions make cigarettes cheaper, which can be especially important to kids who usually don't have much money. Promotions make it easier for kids to afford their first (and second and third) packs. Cheap packs might be just the prod a teen needs to experiment with cigarettes. They might also prompt an experimental smoker to become a habitual one. When the price of Marlboros, the favorite brand of teens, was slashed in 1994, for example, sales soared, from less than 20 percent of the market share to 28 percent.[13]

Specialty Items and Catalog Promotions

T-shirts, caps, wallets, charm bracelets, temporary tattoos, fancy lighters, duffel bags—all bearing a brand logo—are distributed by tobacco companies through the mail or at special promotional events. By saving the bar codes or certificates (e.g., Camel Cash, Marlboro Miles) on cigarette packs, consumers can trade them for items slickly displayed in catalogs. A Swiss Army field watch, for example, can be had for 1,450 Marlboro Miles through the Marlboro Country Store. Philip Morris has even sent vans to convenience store parking lots, where customers "cash in" their Miles on-site.[14] Prefer something in denim? Joe's Biker Jacket (with Joe himself embroidered on the back) goes for 490 C-Notes in the Camel Cash Catalog.

Order forms for coupon redemption require a birth date and a signature certifying that the participant is at least twenty-one years old and eager to "receive offers, premiums, coupons, or free cigarettes that may be sent to me in the mail."[15] In small print is a message saying that giving false information may be in violation of law. Yet minors seem to have no trouble redeeming coupons and acquiring merchandise. In a 1992 Gallup poll of 1,125 American teens, half of the smokers and a quarter of the nonsmokers said they owned at least one promotional item from a tobacco company.[16]

Effect on Teens: By getting and using logo-bearing gear, teens become, in effect, walking advertisements without warning labels. As such, cigarette promotion can stroll down school hallways or attend football practices—places off limits to standard types of cigarette advertising.

Seeing peers in Camel apparel or toting Marlboro duffels, again, makes smoking appear more pervasive than it in fact is (remember, even nonsmokers own promotional items). It also reinforces smoking, as kids wish to be one of the crowd and to own such stylish stuff. One denim jacket requires buying 3,200 cigarettes—a pack a day for almost half a year.[17] A Baltimore teen has a friend so enthusiastic about brand-name gear that "he'll smoke a couple of packs a day" and steal extra coupons just to get it.[18]

Free Samples

Each year the industry spends about $100 million giving ciga-rettes away in public places. Although deemed "for adults only," there's little control over who actually gets the smokes.

Effect on Teens: If a young person gets free cigarettes, chances are he or she will smoke at least a few of them, especially if the distribution takes place where smoking is allowed. Basically, this is a straightforward means of putting free samples of an addictive product into the hands of potential smokers.

Says Mark Green, New York City commissioner of consumer affairs: "Fifty years ago, my late father, Irving Green, was handed a free pack of Camels by a tobacco company representative during a break in the middle of a college exam. In his opinion, this one 'gift' got him addicted for half a century."[19]

Direct-Mail Promotions

Tobacco companies spend more than ever, about $65 million in 1991, in direct-mail promotions.[20] Companies compile mailing lists from coupon redemptions and smoker surveys to send out special offers and magazines (with even more ads and coupons). The Philip Morris mailing list, for example, had 26 million names in 1993, about 1.6 million of them American teens.[21]

Effect on Teens: Getting coupons, special offers, glossy advertisements, and even actual cigarettes right on their doorstep again reinforces the notion among teenagers that smoking is normal, cool, convenient, and inexpensive.

Sponsorship of Sporting Events and Public Entertainment

Tobacco companies sponsor cultural and sports events, reaching out to large numbers of people with diverse interests. Events include art exhibits, ballets, operas, and concerts of every imaginable type—classical, rock, rap, country and western, blues, and jazz (e.g., the Kool Jazz Concert)—and sports events such as tennis tournaments (Virginia Slims, until 1994, when Philip Morris withdrew sponsorship owing in part to public pressure), high-risk car races (the Winston Cup series, the Marlboro Grand Prix), motorcycle races (Camel Moto Cross), and rodeos.

Cigarette brand names and logos—without health warnings—are ubiquitous at such events. During the 1989 Marlboro

Grand Prix, televised to millions of people, the Marlboro logo was visible for 46 of the 94 total minutes of broadcast time.[22] Viewers saw the word *Marlboro* 5,933 times![23] This is clearly a form of advertising that bypasses federal regulations banning tobacco advertising on television.

By sponsoring performances, races, or teams (e.g., the 1995 Marlboro Team Penske), a brand becomes firmly associated with a particular sport or cultural event. Smoking may thus seem to carry the endorsement of participating athletes or performers.

Effect on Teens: Through such events, tobacco companies reach young people with persistent, warning-free advertising. Although the industry argues that most children and teenagers don't attend or watch these events on television, that's not entirely true. During 354 motor-sports broadcasts in 1992, about 7 percent of a total 915 million viewers were children and teens. Seven percent may not sound like much, but in this case it represented sixty-four million kids![24] Studies show that youths accurately link sporting events with tobacco brands. In a teen's mind, the image of a particular brand as rugged, strong and independent, cool, whatever, is strengthened by this association.

Promotional Allowances and Point-of-Sale Advertising

One-quarter of marketing money is spent on promotional allowances and 7 percent on point-of-sale advertising that puts cigarettes where everyone notices them.[25] Promotional allowances are fees that tobacco companies pay to retailers for display space. For example, a convenience store owner might be paid $8,000 for stocking a company's brands.

Point-of-sale materials, often including current coupon catalogs or buy-one-get-one-free offers, tie in with a brand's national campaign. The retailer wants to sell cigarettes, so the more seductive the in-store advertising displays, the happier the store owner. Cigarettes are stocked at checkout counters, next to candy or snack racks and other places that encourage impulse buying.

Effect on Teens: It's impossible to avoid the eye-catching cigarette displays at checkout counters. Every time a teenager pays for a tank of gas, or every time a child buys a candy bar at the corner store, he or she is exposed to the glitzy displays. Since underage youths have little trouble buying cigarettes, they can easily head home with a pack of Camels as well as a Snickers bar.

THE JOE CAMEL CONTROVERSY

Although the R. J. Reynolds Company denies that its Joe Camel campaign targets children and teens, it certainly attracts them. Before Cool Joe's appearance in 1988, fewer than 1 percent of underage smokers preferred Camels. By 1991, a whopping 33 percent did![26] In dollars, sales of Camels to kids soared from $6 million to $476 million between 1988 and 1991.[27] Older adolescents and young adults were less interested in Camels. In one study, 23 percent of twelve- to seventeen-year-olds chose Camels compared to only 9 percent of eighteen- to twenty-four-year-olds.[28]

Researchers looked at how high-school students reacted to

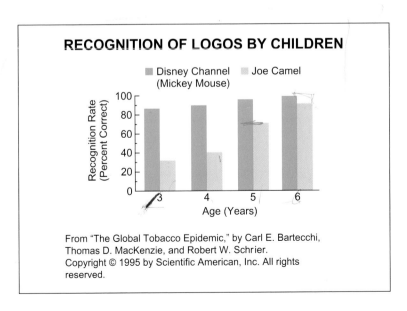

RECOGNITION OF LOGOS BY CHILDREN

From "The Global Tobacco Epidemic," by Carl E. Bartecchi, Thomas D. MacKenzie, and Robert W. Schrier. Copyright © 1995 by Scientific American, Inc. All rights reserved.

49

Joe Camel ads compared with how adults reacted. Students were more likely than adults to recognize Joe (98 versus 73 percent), think the ads were cool (58 versus 40 percent) and interesting (74 versus 55 percent), and find Joe himself a cool character (43 versus 26 percent).[29] In another study, 30 percent of three- and four-year-olds and 91 percent of five- and six-year-olds correctly matched Camel ads with Camel cigarettes from among twenty-two products, including some cigarettes.[30] According to the Surgeon General's Report, "By the age of six, the face of Old Joe and the silhouette of Mickey Mouse (from the Disney Channel) were equally well recognized."[31]

Kids watch cartoons. Kids read comic books. It's hard to believe that the Joe Camel cartoon campaign was designed for adults. The impact of the Joe Camel campaign on children seemed so powerful that the Federal Trade Commission at one time considered forcing R. J. Reynolds to abandon it; after several months of indecision, the proposal was dropped.

THE R. J. REYNOLDS FAMILY

"We've all heard the tobacco industry say there are no ill effects caused by smoking. Well, they ought to look at the R. J. Reynolds family. My grandfather (R. J. Reynolds, founder of the company that makes Camels, Winstons and Salems) chewed tobacco and died of cancer. My father, R. J. Reynolds, Jr., smoked heavily and died of emphysema. My mother smoked and had emphysema and heart disease. My two aunts, also heavy smokers, died of emphysema and cancer. Currently three of my older brothers who smoke have emphysema. I smoked for 10 years and have small-airways lung disease. Now tell me. Do you think the cigarette companies are being truthful when they say smoking isn't harmful?"

—*Patrick Reynolds, in a public-service spot prepared by Tony Schwartz (in* Kids Say Don't Smoke)

ADS THAT APPEAL TO GIRLS

Cigarette brands developed specifically for women were first launched in 1967 with Virginia Slims, Eve, and Silva Thins. Ads were splashed throughout magazines popular with adolescents and young women. Not surprisingly, there was a sudden surge in the number of underage girls who began to smoke that year. By 1973 twice as many teenage girls were smoking than before 1967, while smoking habits among boys remained constant.[32]

Campaigns of the 1970s continued in this vein; the brand names themselves overtly emphasized thinness (Virginia Slims, Silva Thins) or beauty (Eve, with an added element of "forbidden fruit" thrown in). Models were always thin, fashionable, and gorgeous. What young woman—or adolescent—could resist wanting to be like them?

WHAT THE CIGARETTE ADS DON'T SHOW

Janet Sackman was a successful model and cover girl for the magazines *Life* and *Look*. In 1949, when she was seventeen and hired to represent Lucky Strike cigarettes, a company executive suggested she learn how to smoke. "That way you'll look authentic." So she did. Forty years later, she got cancer and had to have first her larynx and then one part of a lung removed.

"Her voice box gone, she had to learn to talk all over again, burping air through a hole in her esophagus just above the collarbone," wrote Anna Quindlen in her *New York Times* column, "Public & Private." Sackman, Quindlen said, yearned to tell teenage girls: "I wish I had realized how important my life was when I was 17. Tell her [a friend's daughter] the single most important thing to do for your looks and your life, the single most important thing, is not to smoke. If she could hear me speak, she'd listen."

—"17 Going On 18," by Anna Quindlen,
New York Times, *November 30, 1994*

51

While today's ads still stress thinness, recent ads for "women's cigarettes" have an additional slant: a female version of the Marlboro Cowboy—a strong, independent, very-much-in-control kind of woman. There's the familiar "You've come a long way, baby" of Virginia Slims and a newer ad for the same brand: "I always take the driver's seat. That way I'm never taken for a ride."[33] Another ad, featuring a Superwoman type (complete with tights and cape), takes a slightly different feminist tack: "We make Virginia Slims especially for women because they are biologically superior to men."[34]

These ad campaigns may indeed have been created for young adult women, but teenage girls are striving to become such thin, strong, independent creatures themselves.

IMAGES OF SMOKING IN MOVIES AND MAGAZINES

Until 1990 tobacco companies routinely paid to have their cigarettes in movies. Sylvester Stallone, for example, received $500,000 for using cigarettes in *Rhinestone Cowboy*, *Godfather III*, *Rambo*, and *Rocky IV*.[35] Even without these "paid product placements," 1990s movies are still hazy with cigarette smoke. Susan Sarandon's character in *The Client* shares a smoke with an eleven-year-old boy. All the cool twenty-somethings (Winona Ryder et al.) of *Reality Bites* exist on coffee and cigarettes. Jim Carrey in *The Mask* impresses a stunning woman by blowing heart-shaped smoke rings. The list goes on and on. Some movie characters may need to smoke to be believable (e.g., gangsters in *The Godfather*, soldiers in *The Longest Day*), but certainly, for example, not the mom in *ET*.

When the National Coalition on Television Violence studied movies from 1987–1988, it found smoking in 87 percent of the PG films,[36] a rate that has been constant since 1960. Although Americans were kicking their cigarette habits during this time, from 42 percent smoking down to 26 percent in 1990, movies clearly did not reflect this trend.[37]

Perhaps more distressing is which characters are smoking

ANGEL IN THE OUTFIELD

Some filmmakers have launched private campaigns against tobacco. Holly Goldberg Sloan, screenwriter for the Disney movie
Angels in the Outfield, for example, embellished a scene where
an angel informs a child that one player isn't long for this world
by adding, "He's smoked for years." Sloan explained: "I resent
that I can drive by a billboard that sells cigarettes with a camel
that my kids think is cute and funny. I wanted to say something
back to the cigarette company."

—USA Today, *June 22, 1994*

on camera. Forty-five percent of young adults in films smoke, although only 26 percent of their real-life counterparts do.[38]
Again, this distortion conveys the message that smoking is more
common than it really is.

Also troublesome is the fact that so many "good guys," the
movie role models for American teens, smoke. Of upper-class
movie characters, 57 percent smoked in films compared with 19
percent in real life. As Stanton Glantz, a well-known researcher,
explains, "The impression kids get from watching these movies
is that most people smoke and smoking is something done by de-
sirable figures. It's not the bad guys who are smoking, it's the
good guys."[39]

Cigarettes are also used as props in fashion and style magazines popular with teen readers. A Guess Jeans model, for example, strikes a sexy pose in *Esquire,* complete with smoldering
cigarette. The young cast of *Beverly Hills 90210* was interviewed
for *Rolling Stone*; the accompanying photograph showed each
star with a cigarette drooping from his or her mouth. Implicit in
the scene is, of course, an endorsement of smoking, an endorsement made all the more compelling by the celebrity of the ac-
tors. Through such pictures, the image of cigarettes as stylish,
sophisticated, sexy, glamorous, and popular is again reinforced.

ARE TEENS INFLUENCED BY ALL THIS HOOPLA?

Since good advertising is subtle, quietly influencing beliefs about smoking, it's virtually impossible to study whether ads actually cause kids to smoke. Few teens would admit being driven to smoking by looking at a few pictures of the Marlboro Man. But tobacco advertising is so widespread, with children growing up bombarded by dancing camels and pensive cowboys, that many kids remember the ads and view cigarettes as part of everyday life. Researchers now know that those who overestimate the prevalence of smoking are more likely to smoke themselves.

Despite the tobacco industry's claim that its ads are directed exclusively at adults, two facts strongly suggest that children and teens are responding to the advertising campaigns.

- Unlike adults, teens consistently smoke the most heavily advertised brands. Marlboro, Camel, and Newport account for 33 percent of overall sales but 86 percent of sales to teenagers![40]

Cigarette brand	Ad costs (in millions)	Market share ages 12–18	Market share USA overall
Marlboro	$75.6	60%	24%
Camel	$42.9	13%	4%
Newport	$34.5	13%	5%

- Soon after the launching of ad campaigns attractive to youth, the popularity of the advertised brands—for example, Virginia Slims and Camels—soars among young people.

—⟋⟍—

What does all this tell us? That tobacco companies spend billions of dollars to appeal to kids, hoping that these kids will fall for their subtle images and get hooked for a lifetime. Unfortunately, all too many kids innocently take the bait and start smoking. That seemingly harmless act, however, has incredibly serious pitfalls, dangers that last—and shorten—a lifetime. Next we'll look at just what the costs are to those kids who fall for the messages the tobacco companies try so hard to sell through the media.

Gabe

Gabe is a fifteen-year-old high-school honors student living near Muncie, Indiana. He says that there's not much of anything he likes about smoking at this point but that he is now physically and psychologically dependent on it, which makes it too hard to quit.

Although he had fooled around with cigarettes at Boy Scout outings since he was twelve, he didn't become a habitual smoker until an acquaintance offered him a cigarette last year, a few months into his freshman year in high school.

"We were competing at the volleyball state finals, and this guy assumed I smoked, and so when he offered me a cigarette, I took it. Ever since then, I've been smoking pretty regularly. In fact, that guy has become a really good friend of mine, and sometimes I tell him I have every reason to hate him because he started me smoking."

Gabe says he was pretty unpopular in middle school and he wanted "to do something to shut people up," and smoking helped do that. Also, music is very important to Gabe; he plays guitar, is proud of his collection of two hundred tapes and a hundred CDs, and has been in and out of bands for several years. Somehow music and smoking have gone together. "I play guitar a lot, and whenever I went to concerts, there were a lot of older guys and I would have felt really out of place if I hadn't been smoking. In fact, I think the only thing I like about smoking is that it opened doors with a lot of people and gave me so many friends. I don't think I would be friends with a lot of my current friends now if it weren't for smoking 'cause it just sort of broke the ice.

"There's not much else I really like about smoking and I really would like to quit but I'm definitely addicted to it. With more than 40 percent of my good friends smoking regularly, it'd be really hard to quit now," says Gabe. He smokes either filtered Camels or GPCs. "A lot of my friends have been smoking a lot longer than I have, and they do not think about quitting, not even as a possibility, and it's getting to that stage for me, too. I wouldn't be willing to give up spending time with my friends [as the price] for quitting."

Gabe is certain that cigarettes are harmful to his health. "I am sure they shorten your life, but that doesn't concern me. But I can feel a real difference in how quickly I become short of breath now, and it really pisses me off."

Both of Gabe's parents, who are in their forties, have smoked for years, and "it definitely is affecting their health." They'd like to quit but just can't do it. "My dad was successful for a month about three years ago. They've both also switched to lights or ultra-lights but still smoke almost two packs a day each. I'm particularly concerned about my dad; I'm afraid he will die young." Gabe's dad knew that Gabe was smoking last year but now believes that he has quit.

Although Gabe doesn't think younger kids would listen, he'd tell them: "I really do regret smoking; it's really bad, but I don't think that would get the point across to ten- or twelve-year-olds. I think I'd tell them how it takes away from so many activities and if they have any inclination to play sports in any way, even recreationally, I'd tell them don't even try smoking because you will have no shot at it whatsoever if you do."

—w—

Gabe started smoking for the heck of it, as something to do with pals. Feeling insecure, he became a habitual smoker after someone he wanted to be friends with offered him a cigarette, believing that he needed to smoke to break the ice. Now it has become an addictive habit much too difficult to break. Although Gabe actually hates smoking and is angry that he becomes short of breath so easily, he doesn't have the willpower to quit. His parents smoke and many of his friends smoke, so he would be the oddball trying to quit. He's basically trapped by age fifteen. He's now worth thousands of dollars to the tobacco companies.

5

WHY THEY CALL THEM "SICKARETTES"

Teens know more about the health hazards of cigarettes than ever before. In 1976 only 56 percent of high-school seniors believed that smoking a pack a day posed a serious health risk. By 1991, 69 percent said that smoking was unhealthy.[1] That still leaves three out of every ten teens thinking that heavy smoking is not hazardous. Many teens learn in school about the dangers of smoking, yet believe they will escape the potentially dire consequences of their habit. They may well be wrong.

People who begin smoking at a young age are more apt than others to become heavy smokers,[2] and heavy smokers are least likely to be able to kick the habit.[3] Those who continue to smoke over the years die younger. It's estimated that every cigarette cuts 5.5 minutes off the life of a regular smoker.[4] That's almost two hours per pack.

Every cigarette smoked, even that first experimental puff, takes its toll on the body, and young, growing tissues are more susceptible to cancer-causing substances than are those of adults. "Smoking causes more death and disease than all other addictions combined. And it has health consequences that start when you smoke your very first cigarette," asserted Dr. Joycelyn Elders, former U.S. Surgeon General.[5]

WHY IS SMOKING SO BAD?

How could such a simple thing—a bit of shredded tobacco, a paper wrapper, perhaps a filter at one end—be so bad? In the case of cigarettes, what you see is *not* what you get. Not visible

59

are chemicals added during the manufacture of cigarettes and compounds produced only when a cigarette burns. Chemical additives (the list tops seven hundred) include heavy metals, pesticides, and insecticides. At least thirteen of the ingredients are not permitted in food; others are so toxic they are banned from landfills.[6]

When lit, a cigarette is anything but simple. At the ash end, temperatures soar to between 1600°F and 1800°F; in the center of the cigarette during a puff, it gets even hotter, up to 2000°F. This intense heat releases some four thousand chemical compounds, including poisons such as carbon monoxide and hydrogen cyanide, mutagens (substances that can cause mutations), and forty-three known carcinogens (agents producing or promoting cancer), including polonium—a pack a day for a year exposes the body to the equivalent of one hundred chest X rays.

As the drive for nicotine compels a smoker to reach for cigarette after cigarette, the deadly substances that are inhaled with each breath are the furthest thing from the smoker's mind. Among the most toxic to human health are carbon monoxide and tar.

Carbon Monoxide

Carbon monoxide (CO) is the poison that killed former tennis star Vitas Gerulaitis, a healthy adult, when a faulty heater released lethal amounts of CO into the air of the beach house where he was staying. The CO took the place of life-sustaining oxygen, and Gerulaitis, in effect, suffocated to death. Yet smokers subject their bodies to CO every time they have a cigarette.

Carbon monoxide is a colorless, odorless, toxic gas produced by combustion. When oxygen supply to a burning material is restricted, CO levels rise—exactly the condition found inside a burning cigarette. Government regulations permit no more than 50 ppm (parts per million) in enclosed spaces, yet CO levels in cigarette smoke can reach 40,000 ppm![7]

Carbon monoxide in smoke passes from a person's lungs

into the bloodstream, where it binds tightly with hemoglobin. Hemoglobin (part of red blood cells) normally carries vital oxygen to all parts of the body and brings carbon dioxide, a waste product, back to the lungs so it can be exhaled. When hemoglobin is bound up with CO, however, the red blood cells can't transport oxygen (or carbon dioxide). As a result, an oxygen shortage may occur.

Although most cigarette smokers do not experience life-threatening CO poisoning because they inhale huge amounts of fresh air along with the CO-laden smoke, they are constantly exposed to this poison. A smoker's blood has from two to fifteen times more CO than a nonsmoker's blood.[8] And smoking in small, closed rooms, especially in the company of other smokers, can raise blood CO to dangerous, even lethal, levels. As CO builds up in the bloodstream, the smoker may feel nauseous, dizzy, short of breath, and headachy. A heart attack is possible in extreme cases of oxygen deprivation. Carbon monoxide can also irritate the eyes and throat and affect vision, hearing, and judgment.

Tar

Tar is also released when tobacco burns. It is comprised of billions of very tiny particles that contain as many as three thousand kinds of chemicals, some of them poisonous and/or cancer promoting. Experiments have confirmed without a doubt that cigarette tar induces cancer in laboratory animals.

Tar collects and clogs the bronchi (airways in the lungs), contributing to cancer, emphysema, and other respiratory

---

A SIMPLE EXPERIMENT

How much tar is delivered to the lungs of a pack-a-day smoker in a single year? To get a feel for the answer, combine one cup of molasses and one cup of water.

---

diseases. It also dulls the senses of taste and smell, diminishes appetite, stains teeth and fingers, and causes bad breath. Low-tar cigarettes are available as a "safer" alternative, but tar is important for the flavor of cigarettes and a smoker's sense of satisfaction. As a result, people who smoke low-tar cigarettes typically compensate for the lack of flavor by inhaling more deeply, taking more puffs per cigarette, or simply smoking more. In the end, they wind up receiving almost the same amounts of tar they would if smoking regular cigarettes.[9]

Nicotine

Nicotine is the most insidious ingredient in cigarettes. While not itself as damaging as tar or carbon monoxide—at least not at levels found in tobacco products—it is the desire for nicotine that drives people to smoke cigarette after cigarette. And in smoking, people inhale the other, deadly substances. A colorless, odorless, oily substance that occurs naturally in tobacco leaves, nicotine is physically and physiologically addictive (see chapter 3).

Nicotine enters the body as thousands of minute droplets riding on the tar particles in cigarette smoke. Inhaled nicotine from cigarettes, about one to two milligrams in a standard brand, passes from the lungs to the bloodstream and races to the brain within ten seconds of inhalation.[10] Within fifteen or twenty seconds, nicotine has reached all parts of the body, even the big toe.[11]

Nicotine stimulates certain body functions. In the first cigarette of the day, nicotine boosts the heart rate by ten or twenty beats per minute and blood pressure by five or ten points.[12] The smoker feels more alert and also experiences a general sense of pleasure—the "kick" enjoyed by smokers. At the same time, nicotine stimulates certain nerves in the spinal cord, which leads to relaxation of many muscles in the body. But after twenty or thirty minutes, about one-half of the nicotine from a cigarette leaves the bloodstream;[13] the pleasant feeling diminishes as the nicotine level falls, and the habitual smoker reaches for another cigarette to supply another "hit" of nicotine.

But if you take repeated doses of nicotine, your body soon gets used to it (becomes tolerant) and you feel less of an effect. In other words, as more cigarettes are smoked during the day, the smoker feels less and less of a physical or mental effect even though nicotine is accumulating. Much of this tolerance is lost overnight, when most of the day's nicotine is excreted. That's why the first cigarette of the morning is usually the most satisfying to a habitual smoker: it provides the initial jolt of nicotine, with its almost instantaneous effects on body and mind.

THE HEALTH COSTS OF SMOKING

So how do these substances—tar, carbon monoxide, the nicotine that keeps people smoking, and thousands of other chemicals— take a toll on human health? Unfortunately, in many and varied ways.

The Shorter-Term Problems

Smoking just one cigarette every few days is enough to trigger ill effects within weeks. These include coughing, wheezing, dizziness, nausea, shortness of breath (dyspnea), phlegm production, bad breath, frequent and severe respiratory infections, decreased physical fitness, and reduced lung function.

RESPIRATORY EFFECTS Cigarette smoke burns the tiny cilia (hairs that line the bronchi and filter out harmful particles) or coats them with sticky mucus; tar accumulates in bronchi; other tiny particles clog the alveoli (air sacs where oxygen and smoke are absorbed into the blood). It's no wonder that the lungs of smokers are compromised. Some teen smokers have abnormal function of both large and small airways. Kids as young as fourteen show abnormalities attributable to smoking within a year of beginning to smoke one or two cigarettes a day.[14] The lungs of many children and teens who smoke never fully develop and never function as well as healthy lungs of nonsmokers.

Young smokers also experience more frequent and more severe respiratory infections, influenza and influenza-like illnesses, and other respiratory ailments than nonsmokers. In one study of boys at a prep school, for example, kids who smoked at least one cigarette a day visited the clinic twice as often as nonsmokers and experienced almost four times the number of severe respiratory illnesses as their nonsmoking classmates.[15]

CARDIOVASCULAR EFFECTS Although heart disease and stroke are rare in teenagers, smoking at a young age can contribute to early onset of life-threatening diseases such as atherosclerosis (thickening of the arteries). Smoking makes blood platelets particularly sticky, thereby boosting the chances of blood clot formation. A blood clot can clog an artery and cut off blood flow to the heart, which can lead to a heart attack; a blood clot in a brain (cerebral) artery can lead to a stroke.

When atherosclerosis does occur in young adults and teens, autopsy studies have linked it to cigarette smoking. In at least two studies of young people, the extent of the disease was directly linked to how much the person had smoked in his lifetime: heavy smokers had more advanced atherosclerosis than did others.

Similarly, in a study of young smokers (ages eight to nineteen), researchers found higher cholesterol levels than in young nonsmokers; high cholesterol is another risk factor for atherosclerosis.[16]

PHYSICAL FITNESS EFFECTS Although many kids don't care how their behavior today may jeopardize their health tomorrow, they might care that smoking can noticeably affect athletic performance and endurance. Simply put, smokers don't make good athletes.

Highly trained athletes have lower-than-average heart and basal metabolic rates, and greater-than-average capacity of the blood to carry oxygen. Cigarette smoking, however, compromises both of these markers of an athlete. Smoking increases heart and basal metabolic rates; and the amount of oxygen the blood can carry is reduced by the carbon monoxide in cigarette smoke. Not surprisingly, studies have shown that smokers can run neither as far nor as fast as nonsmokers.

The Longer-Term Problems

Thirty years ago, when scientists realized that smoking seriously affected health, the first warning label on cigarette packages and advertisements read: "Cigarette Smoking May Be Hazardous to Your Health." For a few years, public health officials believed this label was forceful enough. But as more and more studies revealed increasingly serious effects of smoking, the warning was strengthened. Between 1970 and 1985 it read: "The Surgeon General Has Determined That Cigarette Smoking Is Hazardous to Your Health."

Since 1985, however, one of the four rotating labels has read: "SURGEON GENERAL'S WARNING: Smoking Causes Lung

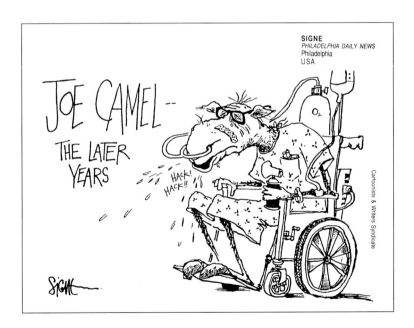

Cancer, Heart Disease, Emphysema, and May Complicate Pregnancy." The statement is finally clear: cigarette smoking *causes* potentially fatal diseases. Heart disease is the number one killer of Americans, cancer is number two. Smoking directly causes 21 percent of all heart disease deaths and 30 percent of all cancer deaths (87 percent of lung cancer deaths).[17]

A few years back, when the annual American death toll from smoking stood at 350,000, a striking image drove home the point: the 1,000-daily death rate was equivalent to three jumbo jets, fully loaded, crashing each day with no survivors.

Researchers now estimate that active smoking causes up to 434,000 deaths every year in the United States; passive smoking kills another 53,000 Americans.[18] Overall, "smoking is responsible for more than one of every six deaths in the United States."[19]

Let's look more carefully at what is killing off smokers at a young age.

CANCER   Smoking causes lung cancer and causes or contributes to cancer of the cervix, larynx, mouth, esophagus, bladder, pancreas, and kidney. Heavy smokers (a pack a day) are fourteen times more likely to die from lung, throat, or mouth cancer than are nonsmokers.[20] Lung cancer has overtaken breast cancer as the leading killer of American women; in fact, women now have about twice the lung cancer risk of men if they have smoked about the same number of cigarettes.[21]

The longer you have smoked, the greater your risk of lung cancer. In one analysis cited in the 1994 Surgeon General's Report, "the risk [of dying from lung cancer] at age 50 for a person who began smoking regularly at age 13 is 350 percent greater than that for a 50-year-old who started smoking at age 23."[22]

About 27 percent of pancreatic cancer (a very deadly disease that kills half its victims within weeks of diagnosis) is also caused by smoking.[23] And once again, the message is clear: the longer you have smoked, the greater the chances of getting pan-

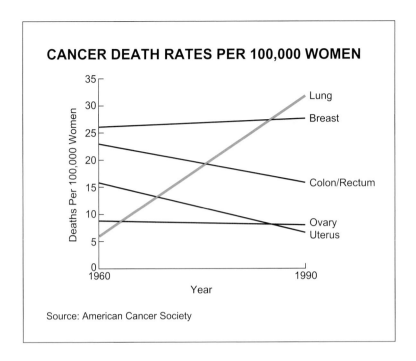

CANCER DEATH RATES PER 100,000 WOMEN

Lung
Breast
Colon/Rectum
Ovary
Uterus

Deaths Per 100,000 Women

Year

Source: American Cancer Society

creatic cancer, according to scientists at the National Cancer Institute.

While breast cancer is one of the few major cancers apparently not caused by smoking, women who smoke are 25 percent more likely to die from breast cancer—once they have the disease—than are nonsmokers.[24]

HEART DISEASE AND STROKE   Three-quarters of a million Americans die every year from heart disease; 150,000 of those deaths are directly related to smoking.[25] Among people under age sixty-five, smoking is linked with 40 percent of deaths from coronary heart disease.[26] Smoking is one of the three primary risk factors for heart disease (high cholesterol and high blood pressure are the other two). Smoking alone triples the risk of death from heart disease.[27] Smoking in combination with another major risk factor quadruples that risk; a person with all three risk factors is eight times more likely to die from heart disease than a person with none.[28]

With smoking contributing to early onset of atherosclerosis and dangerous lipid (fat) levels in blood vessels, "it is likely that the earlier the age at which one starts to smoke, the earlier the onset of coronary heart disease."[29]

Smoking is also responsible for 18 percent of all deaths from stroke.[30] Women who take birth control pills are warned against smoking (by manufacturers of oral contraceptives, but *not* by cigarette manufacturers); the combination increases the risk of heart attack or stroke death, especially among women over age thirty-five.[31]

RESPIRATORY DISEASES   By injuring the lungs and airways leading to lungs, smoking is the major contributor to a group of respiratory problems known as chronic obstructive pulmonary disease (COPD). Bronchitis and emphysema are two of the most common of the group. Eighty-two percent of all COPD deaths are caused by smoking.[32] As cilia become irritated and burned by smoke, they can no longer filter out particles. Airways become inflamed. Excessive mucus builds up, clogging air passages and making breathing difficult. Bronchitis sufferers develop a deep, chronic cough, the body's effort to expel the mucus. Those with emphysema have trouble breathing—cigarette tar destroys the elasticity of the lungs, interfering with their ability to expand and contract. Both bronchitis and emphysema are often long-term, disabling diseases. People may suffer for years, with little hope for improvement.

Light smokers are three times more likely than nonsmokers to die from COPD; heavy smokers (at least a pack a day), twenty-two times more likely.[33]

SKIN PROBLEMS   Because smoking constricts blood vessels, blood flow to a smoker's skin is reduced. In addition, certain chemicals in smoke are believed to damage the skin and cause wrinkles! Smokers are four times more likely to have a lot of facial wrinkles than nonsmokers, and to develop wrinkles at a younger age.[34] In fact, smoking apparently accelerates the whole aging process. And we hear the message once again: "For a given level of tobacco consumption, the speed-up in aging is greater the younger one starts smoking."[35]

By reducing oxygen levels in the blood, smoking may also slow down the body's ability to heal.

FERTILITY PROBLEMS Smoking also interferes with the ability to reproduce. Women who smoke may have irregular menstrual cycles and are three times more likely to have trouble becoming pregnant.[36] Women who smoke go through menopause about three years earlier than nonsmokers, shortening their reproductive life and putting them at greater risk for osteoporosis.[37]

Cigarette smoking can also affect a male's sperm, increasing the chances of abnormalities and reducing sperm count and speed. Even among otherwise healthy young men, smoking increases impotence by at least 50 percent.[38]

SMOKING AND PREGNANCY

One label on cigarette packages reads: "SURGEON GENERAL'S WARNING: Smoking by Pregnant Women May Result in Fetal Injury, Premature Birth and Low Birth Weight." In other words, smoking while pregnant can harm or even kill the baby. In fact, one out of every ten fetal and infant deaths in the United States is linked to smoking.[39]

How? Because the toxins in cigarette smoke (e.g., nicotine, carbon monoxide, hydrogen cyanide) that enter a mother's bloodstream also cross the placenta to the blood of the unborn child. These toxins increase the risk of birth defects, miscarriage, and stillbirth. Carbon monoxide prevents a fetus from getting all the oxygen it needs, contributing to slower-than-normal growth. A pregnant woman who smokes two packs of cigarettes a day deprives her baby of about one-fourth of its normal amount of oxygen, according to one researcher.[40] Others stress that "the time has come to recognize cigarette smoking as the single most powerful determinant of poor fetal growth in the developed world."[41]

As a result of the slower-than-normal growth, smokers are twice as likely to have low-birth-weight babies, a condition that puts babies at risk for a host of medical complications.[42] Low birth weight has been called the "single most important predictor of neonatal [newborn] morbidity and death."[43]

After birth, babies of mothers who smoke during and after pregnancy are much more likely to die from sudden infant death syndrome (SIDS). One study of two hundred SIDS cases concluded that a baby exposed to smoke from more than twenty-one cigarettes a day was twenty-three times more apt to die than a baby exposed to no smoke at all.[44] Mothers who breast-feed their infants and also smoke not only produce less milk but produce milk that contains toxins from cigarette smoke.

To make matters worse, children whose mothers smoked during pregnancy have lower lung capacity than others; this damage is irreversible. There is also evidence that smoking during pregnancy contributes to various childhood or adult cancers, leukemia, cleft palate and other birth defects, hearing impairment, and delayed development during childhood. Some doctors call smoking during and after pregnancy a form of child abuse.

THE ILL EFFECTS OF SECONDHAND SMOKE

Smoke not only robs the smoker's body of robust health but also affects people nearby. Friends and family near a smoker inhale "secondhand" smoke (also called environmental tobacco smoke, or ETS) wafting from a smoldering cigarette (sidestream smoke) or blown out by the smoker himself (mainstream smoke). Sidestream smoke is by far the major contributor to ETS. Typically, a smoker takes ten puffs a cigarette, two seconds per puff, over the course of the ten or so minutes a cigarette is burning.[45] For the twenty seconds of direct smoking "enjoyed" by the smoker (inhaling mainstream smoke), anyone around inhales 9.5 minutes of sidestream smoke, that is, the smoke that curls up from the end of the cigarette.

Secondhand smoke is nasty stuff. It contains more particulates than mainstream smoke (after all, it's not filtered) and has higher concentrations of some toxic substances — including carcinogens, such as benzene. While it's true that passive smokers inhale a mixture of smoke and air, not just smoke, the "cigarette equivalents" can be startling.

Katharine Hammond, an environmental health expert, analyzed the ETS exposure of a nonsmoking office worker after a month with smoking colleagues. Hammond found that "in that same room, at that same time, the nonsmoker is getting as much benzene as a smoker gets in smoking six cigarettes; as much 4ABP (4-Aminobiphenyl), a known human carcinogen, as if smoking 17 cigarettes; and as much NDMA, the potent animal carcinogen, as one who smoked 75 cigarettes."[46]

In January 1993 the Environmental Protection Agency identified ETS as a Class A — very potent — carcinogen, in the same league with other highly toxic carcinogens such as asbestos, benzene (a constituent of ETS), and radon, all known causes of cancer in humans. The EPA concluded that "the widespread exposure to environmental tobacco smoke in the United States presents a serious and substantial public health risk."[47]

Effects on Children

"Bringing up a child in a smoking household is tantamount to bringing him or her up in a house lined with asbestos and radon," says Dr. William G. Cahan, surgeon at a cancer center (who calls his operating room "Marlboro Country").[48]

Children growing up around smokers are twice as likely to get respiratory infections (e.g., bronchitis, croup, pneumonia, chronic cough, and wheezing) and asthma than children in smoke-free homes.[49]

But the effects of ETS on children aren't always as obvious as a cough or an asthma attack. Children growing up around smoke lose some lung capacity or function, which is irreversible and still evident years later. Researchers have found evidence of nicotine and carcinogens in youngsters whose moms were light smokers (ten or fewer cigarettes per day) and worse (higher) than normal cholesterol levels in children and teens. Almost three million American children already have high cholesterol levels; passive smoke is putting them at even higher risk of eventual heart disease.

Today nine million preschoolers live with at least one smoker. Some nonsmoking parents have sued for child custody during divorce proceedings, claiming that their smoking ex-husband or wife is putting the child at risk by exposing them to ETS.

Effects on Adults

Passive smoking is now the third major preventable cause of death in the United States, following active smoking and alcohol-related deaths. More people die from effects of ETS than from car accidents or homicides.[50] Most of the ETS-related deaths are not from cancer but from heart disease: by one estimate, ETS causes 47,000 annual deaths from heart disease and another 150,000 nonfatal heart attacks.[51] Three thousand lung cancer deaths per year are blamed on secondhand smoke, making ETS the third leading cause of lung cancer (behind active smoking and indoor radon).[52]

—⁂—

Thus the health costs of teen smoking are extremely high. People who smoke or live around smokers get sicker and die sooner than people in smoke-free environments. Those who begin smoking in their teens and smoke for years are most likely to be the victims.

But teen smoking has other costs: economic costs.

Brandon

Brandon, a fifteen-year-old in Seattle, started smoking at age twelve when his mother and ex-stepfather were going through a divorce. "I was really stressed and my friend was smoking, and when he gave me one, it calmed me down." He says he doesn't think he's addicted now, but smoking has definitely become a habit. He smokes almost a pack a day of Marlboros or Camels.

Although Brandon plays sports whenever he can, including team football, basketball, and baseball, he says he thinks that smoking has probably only slowed him down a little; since he is still performing very well—running seven-minute miles—he's not particularly worried. All his friends smoke, and he feels that smoking "mellows" him when he gets stressed.

Brandon did quit once for about four months during football season. "We were playing a lot of ball in the snow and it got harder to run. But then a lot of personal things started happening, and I felt stressed again and went back to smoking." He still thinks about quitting sometimes, especially during a sports season, but then he'll feel stressed again and will want to smoke.

He knows that cigarettes are bad for him, but he says smoking, like many things, has both advantages and disadvantages and he doesn't really worry about its potential health hazards, believing that he could quit at any point if he wanted to. He thinks a lot of kids his age smoke out of peer pressure; a kid will smoke to blend in with a group of kids who smoke. "I also think kids smoke because they're under a lot of stress."

Both his mother (she started at age thirteen) and his biological father smoke. His mother doesn't care if he smokes in the house, but his father, who still smokes, won't admit that his son does and won't allow it in his house.

Despite his own habit, if he were to advise a younger kid, Brandon would say, "Do not have that first cigarette. It's not worth it, no matter what anybody says. It just drains your bank account. It's like a drug, and it puts a hole in your pocket and you won't have any money left for anything else. At times, I regret ever starting, but I think I could still quit if I wanted."

—⁂—

Brandon started smoking without thinking much about it. He felt stressed and wanted to do something that he thought might help. Both his parents smoked, and most of his friends smoked, and trying it himself seemed somewhat natural. Because he does not detect any health problems due to smoking now, he does not think about what smoking may be doing to his long-term health. And like many teens, he believes he could quit if he wanted to. Unfortunately, he's probably wrong.

6

BIG BUCKS UP IN SMOKE:
THE ECONOMIC COSTS OF SMOKING

Although the price of cigarettes varies widely by brand, type, and taxes, a typical pack costs about $2.00. That doesn't seem like much money for twenty cigarettes, about 10¢ apiece. But few smokers—teens or adults—are content with a pack a month, or even a pack a week. Those $2.00 packs quickly add up to hundreds or thousands of dollars. And because of its damaging effects on health and safety, smoking has become much more than a simple personal expense—some costs of smoking, billions of dollars' worth in fact, are borne by society as a whole.

THE COST TO TEEN SMOKERS

Americans buy more than 500 billion cigarettes every year.[1] Of those, teens under eighteen smoke an estimated 17 billion.[2]

To support a typical pack-a-day habit, U.S. teens spend some $700 to $800 a year each. With minimum wage at $4.25, a teen smoker must work three and one-half hours a week just to sustain a cigarette addiction. It's easy to think of other ways to spend that much money:

- Treat forty friends to a movie, followed by nineteen pizzas (with every topping imaginable) to eat while reading 162 comic books.[3]
- Play seven or eight video-arcade games every day of the year.
- Buy a top-of-the-line mountain bike plus accessories.
- Add $60 worth of new clothes to your closet every month.
- Buy a new paperback book or two each week of the year.

- Fly to some fabulous vacation spot for spring vacation.
- Or deposit $700 every year in a bank account; at 5 percent interest, after twenty years you'd have $25,000.[4] That's enough for a couple of years of college, the down payment on a house, start-up costs for a small business, or a fancy new car.

And since cigarette prices keep climbing—a pack cost only 23¢ in 1955[5]—it's certain they will continue to rise. In a few years that annual $700 for cigarettes could easily be $1,000.

THE COST TO ADULT SMOKERS

If a teen started smoking at age fifteen and smoked a pack a day for thirty years, he or she would have spent some $25,550, not to mention inflation or how much could have been earned if the money had been invested. But adults pay a lot more to smoke than just the out-of-pocket cost of cigarettes. These costs range from higher health care costs—on average, male smokers spend 28 percent and female smokers 21 percent more than nonsmokers for lifetime medical care[6]—to higher insurance premiums.

Since a smoker is apt to die at a younger than normal age, smokers pay higher life insurance premiums than do nonsmokers. For example, a nonsmoker taking out a $100,000 term life insurance policy with Mutual of New York would pay a total of $25,000 between the ages of twenty-five and seventy. A smoker, in contrast, would spend $39,600 for that same policy.[7] Insurance companies are simply heeding statistics: male smokers (ages thirty-five to sixty-four) are 3.7 times more likely to have a stroke and 2.8 times more likely to have heart disease than nonsmokers; female smokers are 4.8 times more likely to have a stroke, 3 times more likely to have heart disease.[8]

Smokers also pay extra (5 to 10 percent more than nonsmokers) for car and homeowner's insurance.[9] Insurance companies are well aware that smokers get in more car crashes (perhaps because they take risks besides smoking, such as drinking and driving, driving without a seat belt, or speeding) and have more frequent and more deadly house fires than their nonsmoking counterparts.

Miscellaneous expenses add up, too: stained teeth to bleach, mouths to freshen, carpets to clean, houses to ventilate, and clothes and furniture with burn holes to replace or repair.

COSTS TO SOCIETY

Although estimates on the dollar value of the nation's smoking habit vary widely, price tags range from $50 billion[10] to $88 billion[11] for smoking-related health care alone. The Centers for Disease Control (CDC) conducted a comprehensive analysis in 1994 and concluded that health care costs for smoking-related illnesses were *at least* $50 billion in 1993.[12]

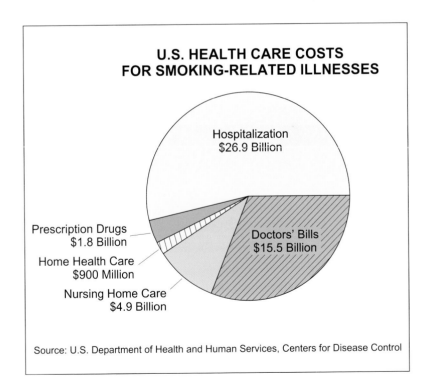

U.S. HEALTH CARE COSTS FOR SMOKING-RELATED ILLNESSES

Hospitalization $26.9 Billion

Doctors' Bills $15.5 Billion

Prescription Drugs $1.8 Billion

Home Health Care $900 Million

Nursing Home Care $4.9 Billion

Source: U.S. Department of Health and Human Services, Centers for Disease Control

The CDC researchers said their figures were conservative, "very minimum estimates."[13] Among their other findings:

- At least 7 percent of all health care costs in the United States are for treating smoking-related illnesses.
- Federal and state governments pay for more than 43 percent of all medical expenses attributed to smoking, and more than 60 percent of those expenditures are for people older than sixty-five.[14]
- Another way of expressing the $50 billion health care total is as cost per pack of cigarettes sold: $2.06. In other words, every pack of cigarettes sold in the United States results in smoking-related medical bills of $2.06. Of this $2.06 per pack, 89¢ is billed to taxpayers, mostly to cover Medicaid and Medicare benefits.[15]

The total bill climbs even higher, up to $100 billion, when estimated costs associated with smokers' sick days ($6 billion), lost productivity ($29 billion), and early deaths ($40 billion) are included.[16] If you also consider factors such as treatment of burns from cigarette-related fires, ailments caused by secondhand smoke, care of low-birth-weight infants, and so on, the costs are even greater.

The bottom line, according to the CDC, is that "smoking-related diseases have an enormous economic impact."[17]

The Tobacco Institute's Defense

The Tobacco Institute, which is funded by the major American tobacco companies and handles their lobbying and propaganda activities, argues that these costs to society are misleading. It reports that a pack of cigarettes costs the U.S. economy just 33¢ before taxes and that smokers themselves pay (through insurance or other means) for all but 49¢ of the $2.06 per pack cost of medical care.[18] This much lower estimate takes into account certain financial "benefits" of the early deaths of smokers.

78

According to a Congressional research economist, one pack of cigarettes costs the nation

- 49¢ for medical expenses that aren't paid by smokers (through insurance or other means)
- 1¢ for excess sick leave
- 10¢ for excess fire and life insurance premiums
- 12¢ in tax revenues lost because of smokers' early deaths[19]

The Tobacco Institute reminds us, however, that smoking results in "savings," too:

- 33¢ per pack in Social Security and pension plans not paid out because smokers die early
- 6¢ per pack for nursing home care not needed[20]

The net cost to taxpayers is thus 33¢ per pack, according to this analysis.

Truth is, smokers do—through taxes and insurance premiums—pay for some of the financial burden their habit imposes on the country's economy. Smokers do die at a younger than average age, at a savings to the Social Security system and other retirement funds. Nevertheless, taxpayers continue to carry a heavy financial load to support smokers, not only in skyrocketing health costs but in ways we usually don't consider when thinking about smoking; these include compromised productivity, building maintenance, and fires.

Smoking and Decreased Productivity

Many smokers are less productive than nonsmokers during a normal working day. According to the *ASH Smoking and Health Review*, employees who take regular cigarette breaks (an average of thirty minutes per day)[21] work almost one month less per year than their nonsmoking peers, at a cost of $29 billion per year.[22] In addition, smokers often get sick, using 34 percent more sick time than nonsmokers.[23] Very heavy smokers (at least two packs a day) miss even more days of work, as much as 84 percent more

---

WHERE THERE'S SMOKE THERE'S FIRE

Mark and a friend had enjoyed several smokes late one afternoon in Mark's upstairs bedroom. Realizing it was time for Mark to leave for his part-time job at a nearby grocery store, both teens hurriedly extinguished their last cigarettes and headed out the door. Mark's dad dropped him off at work and returned home forty minutes later to find smoke billowing out of the house. The structure was saved, but the family's clothes, furniture, and other possessions were destroyed by flames, smoke, and water. Repairs to the house would take months; Mark and his parents had to rent an apartment some distance away. The cause of the fire? One of those last cigarettes hadn't been snuffed out completely. It ignited a couch and the blaze spread from there. Not a pleasant memory for Mark to live with.

---

than their nonsmoking co-workers.[24] Nationwide, some $8.4 billion could be saved with an end to smoking-related absenteeism.[25]

Employers can legally discriminate against smokers, choosing to hire nonsmokers over smokers, and may save millions of dollars in increased productivity, plus lower health and fire insurance premiums, fewer disability benefits, slower depreciation of equipment and furniture, lower cleaning costs, and smaller energy and air-conditioning bills.

Smoking and Building Maintenance

Nationwide, smoking costs between $4 billion and $8 billion each year for building maintenance.[26] In places where smoking is allowed, air filters must be cleaned and changed frequently; carpets, curtains, and windows require regular washing; smoke-stained walls need repainting; ashtrays need emptying. Since the Scott Paper Company banned smoking in the early 1990s, it has saved $200,000 a year in maintenance costs.[27] More and more businesses are waking up to the savings that smoke-free buildings can offer (more than half of the nation's offices were smoke-free by 1994). The savings realized can get passed on to owners, employees, and customers alike.

Smoking and Fires

Smoking is the chief cause of fire fatalities in the United States; one-quarter of all fire deaths in homes are the direct result of lighted cigarettes and other tobacco products.[28] In 1991 alone, 187,100 fires were caused by lighted cigarettes, cigars, or pipes. These fires resulted in 951 deaths, 3,381 injuries, and property damage of $552 million, not to mention immeasurable personal anguish and loss.[29]

INCOME FOR GOVERNMENT: TOBACCO TAXES

Although smoking costs society and smokers a lot of money, smoking also generates money. The tobacco industry supports hundreds of thousands of jobs (in farming, manufacturing, distribution, sales), and excise taxes on tobacco products in 1993, for example, raised more than $12 billion for federal, state, and local governments.[30] The vast majority of this total—98 percent—came from taxes on cigarettes. Though many teens are exempt from having to pay income and other government taxes, they shell out $240 million each year in taxes on cigarettes; more than half of that total comes from illegal sales to minors.[31]

Ever since the Civil War, tobacco taxes have been used as a way to raise extra cash for the nation during wartime or economic depression. In 1898, the tax was 3¢ per pack[32] and held constant at 8¢ a pack from the Korean War in 1951 until the 1980s.[33]

Recent Trends

Since the early 1980s, the federal excise tax on tobacco has been used to help reduce the mushrooming budget deficit. With this goal in mind, Congress adopted several tax increases; by 1993 the excise tax stood at 24¢ per pack.[34]

Despite climbing tax rates on cigarettes, money produced by the tobacco excise tax represents a smaller and smaller portion of federal revenue. Prior to 1913 (the year of the advent of the federal income tax) tobacco taxes provided 20 percent of the government's revenue.[35] In 1950 tobacco taxes represented only 3 percent of total revenues, and by 1989 a mere 0.44 percent.[36]

State and Local Taxes

All fifty states and hundreds of localities impose their own taxes on cigarettes. The District of Columbia commands a high of 65¢ per pack while Virginia, a tobacco state, levies a low of 2.5¢.[37] In general, rates rise—as do many taxes—with a state's need for revenue.

In recent years, however, tobacco taxes have been used not only to raise money for government but also as a way to discourage smoking by making cigarettes more expensive. California voters took the tactic a step further. In 1988 they approved a measure that not only hiked the cigarette tax from 10¢ to 25¢ but allocated 20 percent of that additional income to an anti-smoking campaign.[38] The leading tobacco-producing states (North Carolina, Kentucky, Tennessee, South Carolina, and Virginia), on the other hand, maintain very low taxes (5¢, 3¢, 13¢, 7¢, and 2.5¢ per pack, respectively).[39] Clearly, these states do not want to discourage smokers by making cigarettes too expensive.

—◊◊—

Teens reading these huge dollar amounts linked to smoking may think they have nothing to do with themselves, yet teenagers—smokers and nonsmokers alike—also pay a high price for smoking. For every dollar the government or employers spend on health, safety, and lost productivity, there is one less dollar available for government programs such as schools, roads, playgrounds, libraries, or employer-sponsored benefit packages. For every dollar a parent spends on taxes or insurance to help foot

82

society's smoking-related bills, there is one less dollar available for the family to spend on clothes, food, education, vacations, and recreation. And as soon as teenagers start working themselves, they, too, start paying taxes and help foot smoking-related bills, and there's less money in the paycheck.

Truth is, smoking takes an exceedingly high financial toll on society. Yet such high costs do little to discourage the one million teenagers who start smoking every year from picking up one of the most difficult-to-break habits in the world.

Catelyn

Catelyn, fifteen, is a junior in a high school that's right in the middle of tobacco country in Kentucky. She knows lots of people who make a living from tobacco and sees lots of people smoke around town.

A "B" student, Catelyn works hard; she has a regular baby-sitting job several days after school, does the statistics for the girls' basketball team, and belongs to several clubs after school.

"I guess I smoked my first cigarette when I was twelve. I used to spend summers at my grandpa's house, and one day I took a few of his cigarettes and smoked them in the woods just to see what they were like," recalls Catelyn. "Then I did it more often, probably every couple of days. There was never anything to do there, so I'd sneak some of his cigarettes just for fun."

These days, Catelyn smokes on weekends; about three-quarters of her friends do the same. They only smoke on weekends when they get together or go to parties. "On a typical weekend, I smoke less than a pack. We always pick Marlboro Lights."

In Kentucky, kids have to be eighteen to purchase cigarettes, but Catelyn says all the kids know where they can buy them without any hassle.

Although Catelyn knows her other grandfather died of lung cancer from smoking cigarettes, that her father went to a lot of trouble to quit smoking himself, and that one of her best friends who started as a weekend smoker like herself now smokes every morning and afternoon and is addicted, Catelyn says she's not worried about getting addicted herself.

"I've gone a couple of months, even almost a year, without smoking. It doesn't bother me. I can smoke just when I feel like it."

Catelyn says she knows cigarettes are bad for her. She remembers the anti-smoking education she got in elementary school. She says she can justify smoking to herself because she does it only once in a while. "I know it's bad, but there are other bad things I could be doing instead," she says.

"I like how it relaxes me. Cigarettes don't make me feel good afterward, but during a smoke it relaxes me. That's really all I like about smoking. I don't like how it tastes or what it leaves afterward, or what it smells like, just that it relaxes me. But I don't want to do it all the time, so I don't."

But isn't she scared of addiction? After all, scientists *have* confirmed that nicotine is addictive. "Nah, I'm not really worried that my body will get addicted because I don't do it often enough."

What would she tell younger kids about cigarettes? "I'm sure they want to try them, but they shouldn't do it. Smoking doesn't make them look cool or anything; I don't do it for that. Smoking is bad for you and some people do get addicted at my age; it's not a good thing to do."

Catelyn observes, though, that parents and teachers telling kids not to smoke will not prevent them from smoking. "I don't know what would make people not do it, it's just something they want to do, and if people tell them that they can't do it, that'll just make them want to do it more." The fact that they *are* bad for you, she says, makes it exciting for some kids to smoke because they're doing something they're not supposed to.

Could she stop if she wanted to? "Yeah, I think I could if I wanted."

Well, if she knows she could quit, why doesn't she? She knows cigarettes are bad, but that doesn't stop her from continuing to smoke whenever she gets together with friends. Like a lot of teenagers, Catelyn started smoking as an experiment, to see what all the fuss was about over cigarettes. Most of her friends smoke when they get together, and she has already fallen into the pattern of smoking with them. Like many teens, Catelyn feels invulnerable to the addictive and dangerous effects of smoking. She won't get hooked, she thinks. What Catelyn doesn't realize is that every time she has a cigarette, smoking becomes more and more routine. A habit is beginning to form as she regularly exposes her body to an addictive substance.

One day it's likely that Catelyn will be a daily smoker with not only a habit but an addiction.

HOW SMOKING IS LOSING ITS COOL: SOCIETY'S CHANGING VIEW

*Today, lighting a cigarette in a restaurant is about as socially
acceptable as wandering around spitting into people's salads.*
—Humorist Dave Barry, *in* Kids Say Don't Smoke

Contrary to what the tobacco industry wants us to believe with
its glitzy ads and promotions, most people in the United States
do *not* smoke. Three out of every four American adults and four
out of every five teenagers are nonsmokers.

Public health crusades of the past three decades have been
remarkably effective: whereas 40 percent of adults smoked in
1965, today only 26 percent do.[1] Thirty-four percent of adults
smoked at least a pack of cigarettes a day as recently as 1980;
only 18 percent do so today.[2] The message even reached high-
school kids, at least briefly: 29 percent of seniors reported daily
smoking in 1976, 21 percent in 1980, and 17 percent in 1992.
But the bad news is that this number climbed to 19 percent
in 1993.[3] Almost 30 percent of seniors said they smoked
regularly (within the past month) in 1993, virtually identical to
1980 figures (30.5 percent).[4] Basically, the decline in teen smoking leveled off about 1980 and has remained stubbornly
unchanged—with slight increases offsetting slight decreases—
since. The rate is rising somewhat in the 1990s, causing concern
among public health personnel.

Not only do most people *not* smoke, but most who do smoke

want to quit. According to a 1993 Gallup poll, three-quarters of adult smokers have tried to quit and about the same number thought (unrealistically in most cases) they would give up cigarettes within five years. And about one-third were trying to quit at the time of the survey.[5]

The same goes for teens. In 1993, 74 percent of twelve- to eighteen-year-old smokers had "seriously thought about quitting"; 64 percent had tried at least once to quit, with almost half having tried within the six months before the survey.[6]

But teens in the 1990s are smoking in a very different world than their parents' generation did as teenagers. No longer is smoking widely accepted and commonly permitted. In fact, the last decade has seen extraordinary changes both in how society views smokers and in where these smokers are allowed to light up.

HOW THE TABLES HAVE TURNED ON SMOKING

Smoking was wildly popular until 1964, when the landmark Surgeon General's Report linked smoking with lung cancer. All of a sudden there was a serious downside to this smoky pleasure.

By 1966 cigarette packages carried a required warning label that was strengthened as more diseases—including other kinds of cancer, heart disease, and emphysema and other chronic respiratory diseases—joined the deadly list of health hazards associated with smoking. In 1971 cigarette advertisements were banned from television and radio. These measures targeted individual smokers. Smoking was seen as a medical rather than a social or environmental problem—people who smoked were personally at risk for a wide range of ailments and diseases and were encouraged to quit for their own good.

Nonsmokers Speak Out

In the mid-1970s, however, people grew more concerned about how tobacco smoke polluted the air indoors. For example, nonsmokers who shared offices, restaurants, or bus seats with smokers often complained of stinging eyes, irritated noses, and

"Do you mind if I visibly exhale in your face, dump ashes in your lap, burn a hole in your shirt, smell up your hair, make you sick to your stomach and double your chances of cancer?

From *Tobacco Biology & Politics*, HEALTH EDCO, Waco, Texas.

headaches, as well as the foul and lingering smell of cigarette smoke. Many people felt they had a right to breathe clean air and not be forced to inhale smoke from a nearby cigarette.

Small local groups spearheaded the campaign for cleaner indoor air throughout the 1970s. Although health professionals stayed uninvolved (since there was little evidence then that secondhand smoke posed a serious health threat to nonsmokers), tobacco companies became concerned about this new nonsmokers' rights movement. They hired the Roper Organization to study the situation. A report, secretly issued in 1978, presented some fascinating—and portentous—findings.

- "Most Americans [including nearly half of all smokers] believe it is probably hazardous to be around people who smoke, even if they are not smoking themselves."
- "There is majority sentiment for separate smoking sections in all public places we asked about."

89

- "More people say they would vote for rather than against a political candidate who takes a position favoring a ban on smoking in public places."[7]

The emerging nonsmokers' rights movement was, the report concluded, "the most dangerous development to the viability of the tobacco industry which has yet occurred."[8]

The tobacco industry feared the growing activism for unpolluted air. It didn't matter that researchers had yet to prove that secondhand smoke caused diseases in nonsmokers; what mattered was that people simply thought it was bad to breathe smoke. Even if secondhand smoke were no more than an irritant or annoyance, nonsmokers were becoming aggressive about their right to smoke-free indoor air.

This movement turned smoking into a less socially acceptable activity that was viewed increasingly as antisocial and harmful to others. Smoking had become a social and environmental issue, affecting many more than those who lit up.

Early Legislation

In 1975 Minnesota became the first state to pass a law that required smokers to smoke only in designated areas. The tobacco industry spent millions of dollars trying to thwart similar proposals in other states. These efforts backfired in part because they drew widespread attention to what had been a rather quiet issue. The growing awareness of the nonsmokers' rights issue led to "a strong public consensus . . . that nonsmokers should be protected from secondhand smoke."[9]

Although many statewide initiatives failed to pass, blocked by powerful tobacco lobbies, grassroots efforts such as Americans for Nonsmokers' Rights had success at a local level. In 1982, for example, after a California clean air act had been defeated twice, almost identical laws were passed by several California communities.

In 1983 San Francisco was among the first American cities

90

to approve an ordinance protecting nonsmokers from second-hand smoke at work. The tobacco industry immediately spent $1.3 billion attempting to have the measure repealed. Americans for Nonsmokers' Rights and the American Cancer Society (by the 1980s the medical community had taken up the cause) fought back, with a puny $130,000 budget. Voters upheld the measure, handing the tobacco industry its first major political defeat.[10]

The San Francisco Smoking Pollution Control Ordinance (or Proposition P) was important because employers themselves now handled complaints about secondhand smoke in the workplace. If nonsmokers were not satisfied with potential solutions to problems concerning smoke, then smoking could be completely banned at that particular work site. The widely publicized battle over Proposition P opened the way for speedy passage of many other clean indoor air laws, particularly in relation to the workplace.

The Hazards of Secondhand Smoke Emerge

In 1986 Surgeon General C. Everett Koop issued a report, *The Health Consequences of Involuntary Smoking*, detailing what many people had long suspected: "Involuntary smoking is a cause of disease, including lung cancer, in healthy nonsmokers."[11] A second critical conclusion of the report was that "simple separation of smokers and nonsmokers within the same airspace reduces but does not eliminate exposure to environmental tobacco

---

PROTECTING CHILDREN

"A physician notified child welfare authorities when an 8-month-old baby was suffering serious respiratory problems as a result of her mother's smoking. The Oregon Children's Services Division removed the child from the home, and only returned her when the mother agreed to stop smoking with the help of a nicotine patch."[12]

---

smoke."[13] At long last, secondhand smoke had become irrefutably a matter of public health. Smoking was no longer merely a personal health issue in which smokers damaged their own bodies but a public health issue in which smokers were harming others.

ISSUE OF CIVIL RIGHTS

As evidence mounted that secondhand smoke can cause serious and even lethal diseases in nonsmokers, society has had to grapple with a person's right to smoke versus the right of nearby nonsmokers not to have to inhale potentially deadly smoke. Should smokers have the right to determine their own conduct even if that behavior may have ill effects on others?

The tobacco industry says that regulating smoking on these grounds is an "unnecessary intrusion into private affairs," a "massive intervention in the private lives of adults."[14]

Increasingly, Americans disagree. More and more believe that smoking is no longer "not anyone else's business" because of its high cost to society. Many people now see this unhealthy personal choice as a public concern as well. As researcher Stanton A. Glantz says, "I'm a scientist, and if I see someone putting poison in the water supply, it's only prudent that I act."[15] At the same time, however, nonsmokers need to be supportive of smokers and aware of the difficulties they face in an increasingly smoke-free society.

RECENT MOVES TOWARD SMOKE-FREE ENVIRONMENTS

By 1992 more than five hundred laws had been adopted in different parts of the country, first separating smokers from nonsmokers and more recently banning smoking altogether in many schools, workplaces, restaurants, and public places.

In 1993 the Environmental Protection Agency classified environmental tobacco smoke (ETS: another name for secondhand smoke) as a Class A carcinogen (as toxic as radon and

asbestos), estimating that it causes 3,000 lung cancer deaths annually in nonsmokers.[16] Other reputable organizations—including the Surgeon General's Office, the National Research
Council, the National Institute of Occupational Safety and
Health, and the National Academy of Sciences—had reached
the same conclusion: ETS can cause fatal lung cancer in nonsmokers and serious respiratory diseases in children.

Despite the tobacco industry's attempts to discredit these
conclusions (through counter studies, advertisements, and legal
battles), a flurry of anti-smoking reforms followed the EPA report. California alone passed two hundred local anti-smoking
ordinances in two years.[17] Throughout the nation more and
more public places, many used routinely by teenagers, went
smoke-free.

Schools

In 1994 President Clinton prohibited smoking in most schools
by signing the Pro-Children Act, commonly known as the
Smoke-free Schools Act. It banned smoking "in any indoor fa-
cility that provides health, day care, Head Start, library or educational services to children under 18 years of age," which
receives federal funding from any of several agencies.[18]

Many school districts have taken further steps and prohibit
any tobacco use by anyone on school property or at school-
sponsored events. The prohibitions extend to students, staff,
parents, and visitors in school buildings, parking lots, playing
fields, administrative offices, even bus garages.

The Workplace

Since the 1993 EPA report on ETS, many offices, factories,
hospitals, stores, and other work sites have become smoke-free.
Such restrictions not only improve air quality but reduce
cigarette consumption. A year after the Johns Hopkins Medical
Center became smoke-free, for example, 30 percent of the
smokers had quit; those still smoking smoked 19 percent fewer

93

cigarettes than they had the previous year. Total number of cigarettes *not* smoked at Johns Hopkins because of the ban: four million![19]

Other researchers have found that fewer people smoke at all (anywhere, even at home) when their job site is smoke-free; those who do smoke, smoke fewer cigarettes than their counterparts working at places that allow smoking. If you can get through eight hours without a cigarette, why not twenty-four? And if you can't smoke at work, at least that's eight or so hours a day without a cigarette—that translates into fewer cigarettes per day.

Of course, the passing of these restrictions is not always smooth sailing. In 1994 Maryland, a tobacco-growing state with one of the highest lung cancer rates in the nation, issued (through its Department of Labor) a very comprehensive ban on smoking. The tobacco industry stepped in, involving first the courts and then the state legislature. At this writing, the ban has yet to go into effect.

Restaurants

Fast-food restaurants not only employ teenagers (40 percent of employees are teens)[20] but serve them in large numbers. About one-quarter of fast-food customers are under age eighteen, with one-tenth under age ten.[21] A 1993 report, compiled by the attorneys general of sixteen states, urged fast-food restaurants to go smoke-free to protect their young customers and employees. Taco Bell was first to respond, after a year-long customer survey showed that 70 percent of smokers and 84 percent of nonsmokers reported being offended by smoke in fast-food restaurants. The restaurant banned smoking in all 3,300 of its company-owned restaurants.[22] Other chains soon followed: McDonald's, Arby's, Dairy Queen, Chuck E Cheese, and Dunkin' Donuts are now smoke-free.

California, Maryland, Vermont, Utah, and more than one hundred cities have outlawed smoking in all restaurants, regardless of size and type. Even New York City—long a center of haute cuisine—prohibits smoking (except in separate bar areas) in restaurants seating more than thirty-five people.

Contrary to some people's expectations, going smoke-free has not caused hungry customers to eat elsewhere. In a 1993 survey conducted by the National Restaurant Association, 56 percent of adult customers said they would be more likely to patronize a no-smoking restaurant than one with separate sections for smokers and nonsmokers. Only 26 percent of respondents said they would be less likely to eat at such a restaurant.[23] Other researchers, who studied sales figures in thirteen communities that had banned smoking in restaurants, found no significant drop in total sales.[24] This ran counter to tobacco industry reports of losses averaging 30 percent.

Other Smoke-Free Zones

Many other places that host teens have also jumped on the smoke-free bandwagon:

- Seventy percent of shopping malls in the United States are now smoke-free, including several in northern Virginia (a tobacco-growing state, home to Philip Morris) that actively advertise the benefits of their smoke-free status. They promote a "Shop Till You Drop" theme—drop your risk of lung cancer, of heart disease, of low-birth-weight babies, of respiratory problems, of impaired lung function in children.

- Twenty of the twenty-eight major league baseball stadiums now prohibit smoking.[25] The same anti-smoking bill that governs New York City restaurants also bans cigarettes in seats at Shea and Yankee Stadiums, the National Tennis Center, bowling alleys, and even bingo parlors. Some professional and college stadiums and arenas have banned tobacco advertising as well as actual tobacco use. Madison Square Garden agreed to remove a large Marlboro sign often visible on broadcasts of Knicks basketball games. The Garden will no longer allow cigarette ads anywhere "regularly in a camera's focus."[26]

- Professional athletes can serve as role models whatever the policy of their home stadium or court: as of 1993, minor-league baseball players, coaches, and umpires may no longer smoke or chew tobacco anywhere in the ballpark.

- Virtually all air flights within the United States are smoke-free, as are many international flights. Even on long trans-Pacific flights, Delta, for example, found that passengers favor smoke-free flights 4 to 1.[27] Six other U.S. carriers (American, Continental, Northwest, Trans World Airlines, United, and USAir), plus British Airways and KLM Royal Dutch Airlines, have moved toward eliminating smoking on all transatlantic flights. The United Nations has set a goal of totally smoke-free air travel by 1996.

- More than 80 percent of Amtrak train routes are now smoke-free, with smoking prohibited on all runs of four and a half hours or less. Cruise lines have instituted smoke-free dining rooms.

- Even jails are going smoke-free. In 1993 the U.S. Supreme Court allowed a Nevada inmate to pursue his claim that sharing a cell with a heavy smoker violated the constitutional ban on cruel and unusual punishment.

Effect on Teens

In schools, restaurants, malls, and other places where smoking is prohibited, normal behavior appears to be nonsmoking behavior. And when it becomes virtually impossible to "grab a smoke" during a school day, at McDonald's, or at the mall, teens smoke less.

Tobacco-free schools seem to reduce teen smoking. A 1989 study of twenty-three schools found that schools with no smoking allowed anywhere by anyone, supplemented by programs on smoking prevention and cessation, had significantly lower smoking rates than did schools with more lenient rules and little smoking-related education.[28]

About half of all high-school students have part-time jobs, many of them in restaurants (including fast-food restaurants), offices, stores, and day care facilities, places where smoking is increasingly prohibited.[29] While on the job, they can't smoke and don't see others light up either.

It is to be hoped that teens are getting the message: smoking is dangerous for both smokers and nonsmokers. By not seeing people smoking in such places as restaurants, malls, and airplanes, perhaps teens will come to view nonsmoking as more normal and socially acceptable than smoking. With all the restrictions on where smoking is permitted, teens will perhaps find smoking too inconvenient to start or to proceed beyond the experimental stage of tobacco use.

Tobacco Regulation: What's Going On?

Although restrictions now abound on where you can smoke, tobacco itself has been particularly free of regulations. Other products, from bicycles, coffee, and aspirin to matches, peanut butter, cars, and pajamas, are all regulated by the federal government to make these products as safe as possible. If one proves to be "unreasonably dangerous," it can be banned. Yet most consumer-protection laws specifically exempt tobacco, including:

- The Consumer Product Safety Act, designed to oversee "products that present an unreasonable risk of injury."[30]
- The Federal Hazardous Substances Act, under which the Consumer Product Safety Commission initially had the power to regulate high-tar cigarettes. Congress amended the act to exclude tobacco.
- The Toxic Substances Control Act, which regulates "chemical substances [or mixtures of such substances] which present unreasonable risk of impairing health."[31]
- The Controlled Substances Act, which regulates addictive substances.

Why has tobacco largely escaped regulation? Why is there no government agency responsible for controlling the manufacture, advertising, and sale of tobacco products?

In part, the answer is political: the tobacco industry has enormous amounts of money and therefore can influence politicians to oppose anti-tobacco legislation. In part the answer is practical: if tobacco were regulated under any existing law, strict interpretation of that law could mean a total ban on tobacco products. Such a ban would be highly unpopular and virtually unenforceable. The debate is over regulation, not prohibition.

David Kessler and the FDA

Until recently, the Food and Drug Administration (FDA) maintained that cigarettes and other tobacco products were used only "for smoking pleasure" and were not drugs in the strict sense of the term. To be classified as a drug, it must be shown that manufacturers *intend* their product to "affect the structure or function of the body."[32] Since tobacco was considered neither food nor drug, the FDA had no say over its production, manufacture, or use.

In 1994, however, David Kessler, the FDA commissioner, reevaluated the FDA's stand on tobacco. His agency could have the authority to regulate cigarettes if (1) cigarettes were shown to be addictive and (2) companies intentionally controlled levels of nicotine in cigarettes to keep them addictive. Kessler said there was evidence to support both points and asked Congress to provide him with guidance.

In hearings, tobacco executives insisted that nicotine was not addictive and that its levels were monitored only for the taste of a cigarette. Kessler countered, pointing to dozens of studies showing that nicotine is at least as addictive as heroin and cocaine, and with information that suggested companies do indeed control nicotine levels to establish and maintain addiction, and have done so in secret for some time.

As of the writing of this book, Kessler and others have drafted a bill. If passed, it would

- require disclosure of the seven hundred or so chemical additives, now considered "trade secrets," in tobacco products (additives have been disclosed only once a year to the Department of Health and Human Services, whose officials are sworn to secrecy. Kessler, who refused to sign the confidentiality agreement, was refused access to the list!);
- reduce levels of harmful additives (e.g., ammonia and ethyl furoid, which damages the liver), or forbid their use altogether;
- require a warning about the addictive nature of nicotine;
- restrict tobacco advertising and promotion, especially ads targeting children and teens;
- control the level of nicotine in cigarettes.[33]

This bill would give the government the ability to regulate tobacco products without instituting an outright ban. By the control of production (additive and nicotine levels) and promotion (new warnings, restricted advertising), tobacco use might be discouraged, and disease and death from cigarettes would presumably fall.

So What Happens Next?

The fall 1994 Republican sweep at the polls hurt anti-tobacco legislation. A Congressman from Virginia, with strong ties to the tobacco industry, became the new chair of the Subcommittee on Health and Environment, through which any tobacco legislation must first pass. The new chair quickly announced that tobacco was already regulated enough. Lacking guidance from Congress, Kessler and the FDA may proceed on their own. However, without strong congressional support, these efforts may gradually wane and disappear.

In August 1995 President Clinton authorized the FDA to draft a wide-ranging set of regulations designed to keep tobacco away from children and teens. Included on the FDA's list are major restrictions on tobacco advertising, promotion, and sales. If fully implemented, these proposals could have a dramatic effect on teen smoking, but opposition is expected to be fierce and time consuming. (Tobacco companies immediately filed suit to block implementation of the regulations; lengthy court battles are expected.)

FROM WIDELY USED TO SOCIALLY SCORNED

In the 1950s smoking was viewed as a perfectly normal, usual, okay, acceptable thing to do. But then again, so was chewing tobacco fifty years before that. At the turn of the century, spittoons were all over the place, even in bars and restaurants, until a tuberculosis epidemic was linked to the pots full of spit and doctors insisted they be removed.

"At the time, it was considered to be outrageous and anti-American to get rid of spittoons," says Mark Pertschuk, executive director of Americans for Nonsmokers' Rights. "When historians look back on this [smoking] controversy in 25 years, they will think it was very strange that there were ashtrays and smokers in bars."[34]

Indeed, the tables have turned on smoking. Smokers now ask permission to light up around nonsmokers or routinely go outside to smoke. Thousands of public places ban smoking altogether.

But there's still a major problem: one out of four adults and almost 30 percent of all teens coming out of high school still smoke cigarettes regularly (19 percent smoke every day)—it's very hard to quit.

—ᴍ—

Next we'll look at how tobacco companies are battling to maintain their profitable business.

100

Matt

Matt is a nineteen-year-old in the Midwest, on leave from the college where he is majoring in political science. An only child of divorced parents, he is living temporarily with his mother, working part-time, and waiting for more financial aid to allow him to resume school. He has seen his father only twice since he was three. Although he usually smokes more than a pack a day of Salem 100s, he has had to cut back to just a few cigarettes a week while he lives with his mother because she is very anti-smoking.

Matt smoked his first cigarette at age fourteen. His girlfriend smoked and wanted her boyfriend to smoke. "So I started smoking right then and there." Smoking became part of their sensuality and an integral part of their sex life. After they broke up, Matt was left with the habit and its association with sex and pleasure.

Last year in college, he started a newsgroup on the Internet to talk about smoking (alt.smoking). He receives up to one hundred messages a day on his E-mail and has become quite friendly with many of the chatters. All told, more than four hundred people participate in the discussion group.

Matt says that he continues to smoke because it feels good both physically and psychologically. "It brings back good memories, jacks me up, and gets me sexually excited as well." The only thing he doesn't like about smoking, he says, is the cost.

What about its health effects? "Oh, it's been proven to be bad for you, but nobody lives forever, and if you can't enjoy life while you are living, what's the point? So many people spend so much time worrying about everything bad for them and they are miserable all the time. Why subject yourself to that? Smoking poses some risk, but I don't worry about it. Risk is involved with everything you do. There are different levels of risk for everything, and I'm willing to accept the risk. It's worth it to me."

Nevertheless, Matt admits that he probably wouldn't be a smoker had it not been for his girlfriend at age fourteen and all the sexual pleasure associated with smoking. "If I hadn't had an experience like that with her I probably would not be smoking."

Is he now glad to be a smoker? "Yeah, it introduced me to a whole side of myself I didn't know before. I was what my mom wanted, but I like the way I am now." He says he has found many others in the discussion group who also associate smoking with sensual pleasure and that link has become a very significant factor in his life.

Matt says he doesn't think he is addicted to the nicotine in cigarettes and could quit if he wanted to, "but that would take a lot of changes if I wanted to." In the meantime, he checks his E-mail every day and continues to smoke with pleasure and without guilt.

—m—

Matt smoked his first cigarette because someone important to him asked him to. He then had a powerful experience with smoking, sex, and romance. Smoking has become a link for him, not only to sensual pleasure but to a large network of computer friends who enjoy smoking and support one another in their habit. Chances are smoking has become an integral part of his self-image and he is unlikely to want to quit for some time.

Teens are highly sexual, enjoy conforming with their friends, and feel invulnerable to the long-term consequences of smoking. It's clear why Matt smokes; it's unclear how he'll ever stop. Despite all his pleasures, however, he admits he wouldn't smoke if he had to do it over again.

TOBACCO: AN INDUSTRY UNDER FIRE

Although few kids realize it when they light up, each cigarette they smoke fortifies a mainstay of the American economy, one that has been highly successful for four hundred years. Tobacco has made a lot of people a lot of money and has provided billions of dollars in tax revenues to governments at all levels.

But now the industry is under attack. No-smoking bans are sweeping the country; lawsuits are piling up; the surgeon general is calling for tobacco regulation; higher tobacco excise taxes will likely be part of any national health care plan; and cigarette ads are slammed for targeting youth. On top of all this, Americans are becoming more hostile to the industry. Seventy-three percent of adults report unfavorable opinions of the industry, and 68 percent support government regulation of tobacco.[1]

How do tobacco companies remain profitable despite all the adversity?

THE INDUSTRY

Two tobacco companies dominate the $47 billion[2] empire in the United States: Philip Morris controls 45 percent of the U.S. market, with cigarette brands such as Marlboro, Benson & Hedges, Merit, and Virginia Slims; and R. J. Reynolds Tobacco (part of RJR Nabisco) controls another 30 percent, with its brands Camel, Winston, Salem, and others.[3]

Despite a temporary setback in 1993, when profits fell 46 percent because of severe price-cutting, the major tobacco companies are enormously profitable.[4] The top six American companies together made a $5.2 billion profit from domestic sales in 1993 (a "bad" year), with Philip Morris and R. J. Reynolds earning another $3 billion from sales abroad.[5] In fact, the industry contributes some $4.2 billion to the U.S. side of the trade ledger, reported the *New York Times*. As the *Times* put it, "Toyotas in, Marlboros out."[6]

Tobacco is the nation's sixth-largest cash crop.[7] It accounts for 19 percent of agricultural income in North Carolina, the leading tobacco-growing state, and a whopping 31 percent of farm revenues in Kentucky. Other major tobacco states are Tennessee (13 percent of farm revenues), South Carolina (15 percent), Virginia (9 percent), and Georgia (4 percent).[8]

The giant tobacco companies support thousands of workers in growing, storing, processing, and selling tobacco. More than 136,000 farmers planted and harvested almost 750,000 acres of tobacco in 1993 for an income totaling $2.8 billion.[9] All told, almost 300,000 workers in just the five states of North Carolina, Kentucky, Virginia, California, and New York depend on tobacco—at least in part—for their livelihood, according to the Tobacco Institute. (The American Cancer Society, however, puts the figure for tobacco-related jobs at 260,000.)[10] A single mammoth Philip Morris USA plant in Virginia employs 9,000 people.[11]

FALLING DOMESTIC SALES
BUT RISING FOREIGN SALES

It's no secret that smoking has declined in the United States. Almost 640 billion American-made cigarettes were sold in the United States in 1981; that figure slipped to 485 billion twelve years later.[12] Likewise, the amount of land planted in tobacco has gone down from one million acres in 1981 to just 750,000 in 1993.[13] How has the industry kept afloat? By diversifying and going abroad.

Philip Morris, for example, also owns General Foods, Kraft, and Miller beer, making it the world's leading manufacturer of packaged goods.[14] In 1993 Philip Morris earned twice as much from its food division ($21 billion) as it did from domestic tobacco sales ($10 billion).[15] RJR Nabisco also has a successful line of foods (brand names include Oreo, Planters, and Life Savers). Thus the tobacco giants are on firm ground at home, whatever the future of cigarettes in this country.

A second strategy for growth is more threatening in terms of world health: increasing cigarette sales to foreign countries. American cigarette exports have more than doubled since 1980, reaching more than 195 billion cigarettes in the year 1993.[16] Exports climb about 6 percent a year and had a value of $6.2 billion in 1993.[17] Japan (where 61 percent of the male population smokes)[18] bought the most American cigarettes in 1993, 55.6 billion, followed closely by Belgium and Luxembourg (together, 51.2 billion).[19] Sales in Western Europe and other industrialized nations are expected to decline, however, as

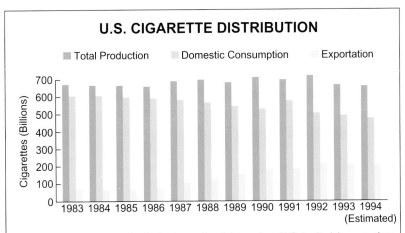

U.S. CIGARETTE DISTRIBUTION

Production figures include distribution to small outlets, such as U.S. territorial possessions.

From "The Global Tobacco Epidemic," by Carl E. Bartecchi, Thomas D. MacKenzie, and Robert W. Schrier. Copyright © 1995 by Scientific American, Inc. All rights reserved.

EXPORTING DEATH

Calculations made by Richard Peto, an Oxford University epidemiologist, "suggest that 50 million Chinese children alive today will eventually die from diseases linked to cigarette smoking."[20]

damning medical evidence is publicized and no-smoking bans become commonplace.

But Philip Morris and RJR are setting their sights on the developing world—on areas such as China, Southeast Asia, Africa, and Latin America—basically, wherever they can spread their message (often without restriction) and peddle their product. China alone has 300 million smokers—more smokers than there are people in the United States—who buy 1.6 trillion cigarettes each year.[21]

Although many countries manufacture and sell cigarettes using native tobacco, American (and European) cigarettes are status symbols. Glossy advertisements and promotions, neon signs, and billboards lure people to the American products. Many ads are aimed at women (most of whom don't smoke; 7 percent of Chinese women smoke versus 61 percent of men)[22] and youth. The tobacco companies insist they are merely interested in getting people to switch from foreign to American brands. If that were true, then why would Virginia Slims be heavily promoted in Hong Kong (with the famous "You've come

TARGETING DEVELOPING NATIONS

Victor Crawford, a former lobbyist (and former state senator from Maryland) now dying from throat and lung cancer, summed up the industry's tactics this way: "Their original plan was to hold the fort [at home] until they could flood the Third World. They've been successful."[23]

a long way, baby" slogan), where only 2 percent of the female population under age forty smoke?[24]

TOBACCO WORKERS AND FARMERS

"There's no company that pays like the tobacco industry," says Kendra Pruitt, accounting clerk at American Tobacco.[25] Figures show she's right. The average annual salary of an employee in tobacco manufacturing was $51,517 in 1990.[26] One acre of tobacco is worth an average of $3,862, more than five times the value of peanuts, the next most profitable crop, and ten times that of cotton.[27]

A disturbing side effect of further declines in smoking would be the consequences to farmers and their families—many have already gone out of business, often selling out to larger operations. There were 512,000 tobacco farms in 1954, but only 137,000 by 1987.[28]

An added headache for tobacco farmers is low-cost imported tobacco. To protect these farmers, Congress mandated in 1994 that cigarettes produced in the United States contain at least 75 percent U.S.-grown tobacco. Like manufacturers, tobacco farmers look abroad for profits. "The future for U.S. growers lies in the export market. That market is a very important thing for us to develop and protect," says a spokesman for the Tobacco Growers Information Committee.[29] That market, however, is flooded with cheap tobacco from Brazil, Malawi, Zimbabwe, and elsewhere.

The tobacco industry evidently contributes to the farmers' plight by not sharing the pie fairly. According to one newsletter, "Between 1980 and 1991 farmers' share of the retail tobacco dollar fell from 7 percent to 3 percent, while the manufacturers' share rose from 37 percent to 50 percent."[30] Manufacturing jobs have also been cut, largely due to mechanization.

Yet we need to remember that we shouldn't sacrifice the nation's long-term health to avoid short-term unemployment, says *Kids Say Don't Smoke*. "If 800,000 Americans work in the tobacco industry [a number reflecting people directly and indirectly involved with tobacco] and 400,000 Americans die each year from smoking, then one American has to die for every two tobacco jobs."[31]

DECEIVING THE PUBLIC?

Disturbing evidence surfaced in 1994 that tobacco companies (1) withheld critical health-related information from the public, (2) developed or began to develop "safer" cigarettes but then conspired to keep them off the market, and (3) may have manipulated levels of nicotine in cigarettes to hook consumers.

Much of this information was presented to the House Subcommittee on Health and the Environment by FDA Commissioner David Kessler and has become the foundation of class-action suits against the tobacco industry.

Withholding Health Information

In 1994 the *New York Times* obtained over four thousand pages of documents that indicated that a major tobacco company's own research showed a link between cancer and cigarette smoke. Unwilling to go public with its findings, the company (Brown & Williamson) contended that scientific research had not proved that cigarettes caused cancer, that it was "only statistical."[32]

Refusing to Market Safer Cigarettes

Secretly, however, industry researchers tried to isolate the harmful components of tobacco smoke in hopes of finding a way to remove them. In 1966 a cigarette that heated rather than burned tobacco, thereby reducing cancer-causing material, was patented by Brown & Williamson Tobacco. The cigarette reduced the amount of secondhand smoke and was less likely to start fires. That cigarette, though, was never publicly sold. The company feared that selling a so-called safe cigarette would make its other brands seem "unsafe" in comparison and thus the

108

targets of lawsuits based on disclosure of the hazards of smoking regular cigarettes. Then, too, B&W thought that consumers might not like the new cigarette and might find it unsatisfying without all the tars that contribute to taste.

By 1979 Liggett & Myers also had a "safe" cigarette but voted not to market it; its inventor was not allowed to publish his work. Most companies, it seems, have come up with a less hazardous cigarette but have withheld the brand from the public "for fear the effect would be to invite lawsuits."[33]

Allegedly Manipulating Nicotine Levels

In his testimony before the House Subcommittee, Commissioner Kessler referred to a 1972 internal Philip Morris memo which advised, "Think of the cigarette as a dispenser for a dose unit of nicotine."[34] The same memo stated that "no one has ever become a cigarette smoker by smoking cigarettes without nicotine."[35] Kessler cited numerous sources leading him to conclude: "Accumulating evidence suggests that cigarette manufacturers . . . may be controlling smokers' choice by controlling the levels of nicotine in their products in a manner that creates and sustains an addiction in the vast majority of smokers."[36]

Litigation

These alleged deceptions have led to many lawsuits. During the 1950s and 1960s most lawsuits by smokers claiming that tobacco had ruined their health were thrown out because there was inadequate proof that cigarettes were harmful.

After it became clear that smoking did cause lung cancer and other serious diseases, the legal focus switched to smokers' responsibility for their own health. Cigarette packages and advertising carried warning labels about the dangers of smoking. Users who failed to heed the warnings, it was argued, were themselves at fault if they got sick. Individuals who claimed personal injury from smoking consistently lost in court. Ironically, the warnings on cigarette packages—which are meant to protect smokers and potential smokers—shielded the tobacco industry from costly lawsuits.

In 1992, however, the Supreme Court eventually ruled (in *Cipollone v. Liggett Group Inc.*, first argued in 1983) that the federal law requiring warning labels on cigarette packs does not protect manufacturers from lawsuits. As a result, several years later, people started joining together in class-action suits against tobacco executives and their companies. Many of these suits claim that tobacco executives deceived smokers. Aware that cigarette smoking could cause cancer and/or that nicotine was addictive, tobacco personnel insisted otherwise. As a result of such deceptions, the smokers were irreparably harmed. Class-action suits are wide-ranging:

- Florida has class-action lawsuits against tobacco companies, seeking reimbursement for Medicaid expenses—about $1.2 billion per year—from smoking-related illnesses. As one lawyer explained, "The taxpayers didn't make the decision to smoke. Therefore, they shouldn't have to pay the cost."[37]
- Likewise, the Mississippi attorney general filed suit in May 1994 to recover state money spent for treating smoking-related illnesses. In its suit the state charged that the industry conspired to "mislead and confuse the public about the true dangers associated with smoking cigarettes" and asked that the companies stop "aiding, abetting or encouraging sales to minors."[38]
- In a suit filed in New Orleans (May 1994) lawyers from fifty firms nationwide sued the American Tobacco Co. (*Castano v. American Tobacco Co.*) for billions of dollars in damages on behalf of all "nicotine-dependent persons, heirs, and survivors."[39] Lawyers accused the company of intentionally manufacturing an addictive product.
- In a lower-profile case, San Diego lawyers demanded that tobacco companies pick up the tab (as much as $1,500 per smoker) for nicotine patches and related therapy of smokers

trying to quit.[40] If nicotine wasn't addictive, the argument went, such treatment wouldn't be needed. And if, as industry memos seem to show, tobacco executives were aware of the addictive properties of nicotine, they should be held responsible for the persistent habits of those smokers.

• Karen Sparks, a Seattle mother of two, filed a class-action suit "on behalf of any parent with a conscience" against R. J. Reynolds Tobacco, claiming its Joe Camel cartoon advertisements were illegal because they targeted young smokers who couldn't legally buy cigarettes. The suit demanded health warnings on all Joe Camel promotional items and a "corrective media campaign" about the dangers of tobacco.[41]

Response of the Industry

These cases have not yet been settled. So far, however, tobacco companies have enjoyed enormous success in court. Since the 1950s some three hundred health-related lawsuits have been brought against the industry; companies have never had to pay a penny to opponents. They expect to win the class-action suits with similar tactics: refusing to settle claims while spending as much money as necessary to win. Industry lawyers argue that companies can't be required to pay "for specific health costs based on general statistics."[42] "They will have to prove what the situation is for each person," according to one RJR lawyer.[43] If the courts agree, producing medical information for every individual covered by a class-action suit may be too time-consuming and expensive for the plaintiffs to pursue. "We expect to prevail in all the class-action suits and underlying claims," said Geoffrey C. Bible, CEO of Philip Morris. "You must remember, we have never lost a case."[44]

Tobacco companies have also initiated aggressive lawsuits, such as against the EPA for its report on secondhand smoke, San Francisco for its strict smoking ban, and an ABC news show for its report on nicotine manipulation; the show has since publicly apologized.

THE TOBACCO LOBBY

Tobacco companies spend millions of dollars to cripple or defeat legislation that would hurt their industry. They contributed more than $2 million to House and Senate candidates in 1992 with the expectation that those members of Congress would protect their interests.[45]

Evidently, the contributions work. The new Republican head of the House Energy and Commerce Subcommittee, for example, has vowed to end the subcommittee's investigation of the tobacco industry and has promised to block other attempts to "embarrass" tobacco companies. And the Speaker of the House, Newt Gingrich, has declared he'll oppose "any tax increase of any kind [including tobacco excise taxes] coming from this House."[46] Such contributions are probably also behind all those consumer protection bills that, for the past twenty years, have exempted tobacco despite emerging studies that cigarettes were addictive and hazardous to health.

Tobacco companies almost certainly had a hand in reducing President Clinton's proposed $1.00 tax on tobacco products, designed to fund his ill-fated national health plan. Congressional representatives from tobacco-growing states objected to such a high tax — despite popular support for a $1.00 rate — and it was trimmed to 45¢.[47]

TOBACCO: WHAT IS ITS FUTURE?

The tobacco industry obviously has a lot invested in strenuously defending its companies and customers. It faces static smoking levels in the United States, low-priced rivals, and the looming threat of an excise tax hike. But it continues to thrive and apparently will do so for the foreseeable future. According to *Business Week* magazine:

> Yet while smoking may be increasingly socially unacceptable, it isn't going away. The economic, legal, and legislative forces that keep the industry strong are too well

entrenched. . . . Like cigarette smoking itself, the U.S. may find that the tobacco industry is a difficult habit to kick.[48]

As smoking continues to harm and to kill, it is largely teenagers who pick up the lifelong habit. In the last chapter, we'll look at possible ways to reduce the toll of teen smoking.

Tory

Tory, a high-school junior in Muncie, Indiana, asked for a cigarette from her friends when she felt very stressed out. "I had heard that it could really calm you down, and it did." She works as a cashier in a busy fast-food restaurant about fifteen hours a week and school is tough; she's struggling to get her grades above a D average. Both her mom and her soon-to-be stepdad smoke. Her grandfather and great-grandmother smoked, but they both died of lung cancer a few years back. After she smoked her first cigarette at fourteen, it took a few months before she was smoking regularly.

"It quickly became a psychological habit that helped to calm me down," says Tory.

Tory said that after smoking a pack of Marlboro Lights every three days or so, she realized that she was staying sick with colds and flu longer than she used to, and that the taste got to be "nasty." She decided one day that when her current pack was gone, she wouldn't buy any more. The pack lasted a week and then she struggled for weeks, using all the willpower she could muster to refrain from smoking. After the first week it got much easier. "My friends can smoke around me and it doesn't bother me at all; I just think, ooh, it's nasty.

"I think a lot of kids smoke because they know it makes their parents mad, and they are rebelling," Tory says. "I'd tell young kids that smoking will make you sick and make you die faster. And it'll cost you an arm and a leg."

Tory says that to keep teens from smoking, she thinks packs should cost $5.00 each, instead of almost $2.00. "That would keep them from smoking."

—

Tory is the exception among teen smokers. After smoking fairly regularly for a while, usually to calm herself down, she began to listen to her body. She was often sick and didn't even really like the taste of cigarettes. From personal experience—two close relatives had died from lung cancer—Tory was also very aware of the long-term devastation smoking could cause. She decided to quit . . . and did. But that was just three weeks before the interview. It would be interesting to talk with her again, and see if she's still smoke-free. If so, that would certainly be an accomplishment.

9

KICKING THE TEEN TOBACCO HABIT

A person who hasn't started smoking by age 19 is unlikely to ever become a smoker. Nicotine addiction begins when most tobacco users are teen-agers, so let's call this what it really is: a pediatric disease.[1]

—Dr. David A. Kessler, FDA Commissioner

As the nation's leading preventable cause of death, smoking needs to become a top public health priority. Virtually all smokers pick up the habit when they are young; only by keeping kids away from tobacco can we reduce the number of future American smokers. Public policy must therefore focus on children and teenagers.

Yet there is no simple solution to the teenage smoking epidemic. "Because influences to smoke are everywhere, our efforts to prevent tobacco use must reach our youth from every source and every angle," said Joycelyn Elders, former U.S. Surgeon General.[2] What can be done?

According to the 1994 Institute of Medicine report, *Growing Up Tobacco Free*, the main strategies are (1) educating children, teens, and communities about tobacco; (2) raising taxes to make cigarettes less affordable; (3) enforcing existing laws against selling cigarettes to minors; (4) clamping down on cigarette advertising and promotion; and (5) regulating the labeling, packaging, and harmful contents of tobacco products.

The following is a broad palette of suggestions that embrace these strategies. With no programs whatsoever, 80 percent of adolescent smokers will go on to become adult smokers.[3] The lives of millions of teenagers are at stake.

EDUCATION PROGRAMS
School-based

As the only place where almost all kids can be reached, schools should be central to tobacco education. The most successful curriculum teaches kids how to resist the social pressures to smoke and includes good communication, decision-making, and problem-solving skills; how to be assertive; health education; the social benefits of being a nonsmoker; and how to "decode" slick cigarette advertisements. Students also learn that most kids *don't* smoke. Programs should also teach about the short-term health consequences of smoking (e.g., bad breath, yellow teeth, and shortness of breath), explore the reasons why kids decide to smoke (e.g., peer acceptance and image), *and* offer opportunities actually to practice ways of refusing cigarettes.

Although trained health teachers and science teachers can be effective, kids talking to kids may be most effective, either same-age peer leaders or older kids talking to younger kids. Such a peer-led program, with role-playing and modeling strategies for coping with social pressures, can reduce smoking 35 to 50 percent more than an adult-led program emphasizing health consequences.[4]

The National Cancer Institute recommends classroom sessions at least five times a year for two years of middle school (sixth, seventh, and/or eighth grades), with "booster" sessions in subsequent years through high school. Classes should be reinforced with strict school policies restricting tobacco use.

Community-based

Other individuals and groups that can tackle the tobacco problem include 4-H programs, youth groups (e.g., Scouts,

YM-YWCA), and Little League baseball and other sports organizations. Local doctors and dentists identifying and working with at-risk students, including school dropouts (70 percent of whom smoke) and absentees, can also be effective.[5]

Communities can make sure that age restrictions on buying cigarettes are enforced and that smoking ordinances and stop-smoking programs are publicized in the local media.

Families can promote smoke-free lives by emphasizing a healthy lifestyle, maintaining smoke-free homes, and helping kids to identify deceptive ads. If a child wants to smoke, families can find an older person suffering from smoking-induced cancer willing to talk about his or her experience. (Ann Landers has repeatedly endorsed the latter strategy.)

Quit-Smoking Programs

Preventing smoking is much more effective than helping kids quit. Smoking prevention programs, unfortunately, have a small and inconsistent effect on kids who already smoke. Often kids aren't motivated to quit but are forced by parents or school officials to participate in a program. Non-school-based programs, such as ones sponsored by health management organizations, have higher enrollments but no better results than in-school programs.

Yet "more than half of adolescent smokers want to quit, try to quit, and fail to quit."[6] Innovative programs now being considered include interactive computer programs, videos specifically developed for kids, and telephone counseling.

RAISING TAXES

Money talks. When Canada raised its cigarette taxes so that a pack of smokes cost $4.22 (in U.S. dollars), teen smoking fell 62 percent.[7] Any increase must be hefty. A 10¢ rise isn't enough, a group of teens told researchers. More than one-third felt, however, that a $1.00 increase would make them less likely to smoke.[8]

Adults, too, can be swayed by their wallets. In one Gallup poll, 64 percent of the smokers said they'd quit smoking if a pack cost $3.00; 78 percent would quit at $4.00; 84 percent would quit at $5.00; and 88 percent would quit at $6.00.[9]

According to *Business Week*, a tax increase of $1.00 would result in 4.5 million fewer smokers, 1.1 million lives saved (people who—if they smoked—would die from their habit), and $14 billion in tax revenues per year. A $2.00 increase would reduce the number of smokers by 7.6 million, save 1.9 million lives, and produce $23 billion.[10]

Yet U.S. cigarette taxes are among the lowest in the industrialized world—56¢ a pack, on average, compared with $3.46 in Denmark, $2.85 in Britain, and $1.21 in Japan (all in U.S. dollars).[11]

Based on evidence from Canada, New Zealand, and Great Britain, the Institute of Medicine panel concluded that "pricing policy is perhaps the single most important element of an overall comprehensive strategy to reduce tobacco use, and particularly to reduce use among children and youths."[12] The panel called for an immediate $2.00 increase, bringing U.S. taxes in line with those of other industrialized countries.

Although more than two-thirds of voters, including one-third of those who smoke, favor a $2.00 tax hike,[13] opponents argue that expensive cigarettes invite black markets, smuggling, and organized crime; unfairly burden the poor, who smoke at disproportionately higher rates; and threaten 300,000 jobs directly related to tobacco. However, moneys from the tax hikes could be used for special programs to aid the poor, for job retraining, and for helping farmers financially as they switch from tobacco to other, nonlethal crops.

Even where a hike in the tax threatens farmers and producers, the impact is likely to be quite small in terms of an area's total economy. Money not spent on cigarettes would be spent on other goods and services.

ENFORCING EXISTING LAWS

Although it's illegal in all fifty states to sell cigarettes to minors, three-quarters of stores do it anyway, raking in $1 billion.[14] Current laws are largely unenforced. Yet perhaps the "biggest payoff at the lowest cost" would come through tough enforcement of existing laws against selling to minors, says Dennis Zimmerman, economist at the Congressional Research Service.[15]

Experts recommend that vendors be required to purchase licenses to sell tobacco, similar to those now required to sell alcohol. Merchants caught selling cigarettes to minors would face stiff fines (current fines, if imposed, are only $100 to $500— nowhere near the profit made from selling to teens),[16] and could lose their licenses for repeated offenses. Without a license, a vendor couldn't sell to anyone, adult or teen. That's a great economic incentive for obeying the law.

Although the federal Synar Amendment mandates that states crack down on sales to minors, states haven't been given any money to cover costs of enforcement. In fact, to judge by the success of community-based efforts, "local governments may be the best hope for effective enforcement of youth access laws," advises the Institute of Medicine's panel of experts.[17] Individual communities can pass restrictions as tough as they please, stricter than their state's. Communities can ban vending machines, enforce laws (with sting operations that test vendors by having teens ask for cigarettes), educate merchants and the public, post signs warning that sales to minors are illegal, and levy stiff penalties.

When one community implemented a model program in Woodridge, Illinois, with retailer licensing, police stings, and hefty penalties for merchant violations, illegal sales dropped dramatically—from teens successfully able to purchase cigarettes 70 percent of the time, to less than 5 percent in just eighteen months.[18] Middle school experimentation and regular smoking fell by more than 50 percent.[19]

120

Similarly, when King County, Washington, instituted some of the nation's toughest youth access legislation, minors' buying success rates dropped from 79 percent to 7 percent in four years.[20]

Either banning vending machines completely or restricting them to bars and other adult-only locations is also highly recommended. Other strategies include prohibiting self-service displays, separating cigarettes from chips and candy bars in stores, minimizing advertising and promotional displays, prohibiting the sale of single cigarettes (which are cheap and less intimidating to buy), and banning free distributions that occasionally take place at rock concerts, fairs, malls, sporting events, and even zoos! Although most states prohibit distribution to minors, this is hard to enforce. Other experts recommend more merchant education about the need to reduce youth access and the importance of their role in achieving that goal.

Ironically, failing to actively enforce restrictions on selling cigarettes to minors actually undercuts other smoke-free efforts. In fact, an unenforced restriction may well be more damaging than no restriction at all. Teens see that adults aren't taking the regulations seriously and figure they shouldn't have to either.

CLAMPING DOWN ON ADVERTISING

Ideally, to reduce teen smoking we'd ban all cigarette ads and promotions that use logos and brand names. However, it's unlikely that such legislation would be approved at the federal level. As things now stand, states and localities are prohibited by federal law from imposing restrictions on cigarette advertising and promotion as long as cigarettes meet federal labeling requirements. If this law were repealed, states and localities could begin to set their own policies. As is the case with youth access enforcement, local initiatives may well have the most impact.

Advertising bans in Norway, Finland, Canada, and New Zealand show us that they can result in significant declines in smoking. A study of thirty-three countries, for example, found that the more governments control tobacco promotion, the greater the decline in tobacco consumption, including consumption by young people.[21] Most effective is a three-pronged approach: education, increase in price, and total ban on advertising.

Other recommendations include restricting promotions and ads on billboards, public transportation, sports facilities, and points of sale; and banning use of trademarks, brand names, and logos in movies, television, and at public events.

REGULATING CIGARETTES

Studies that analyze whether teens actually heed label warnings show that "as far as teenagers are concerned, the Surgeon General's warning is not an effective public health education tool."[22] In one study, for example, only 37 percent of adolescents looked at the health warning long enough to read it; 44 percent didn't look at the warning at all.[23] Current labels are too small, inconspicuous, and are often in colors that blend in with the package or ad. On billboards, warnings are almost impossible to read while driving by. Brand names, however, are noticed and remembered.

Teens still underestimate the long-term dangers of smoking, including the risks of addiction. We need warnings, researchers say, that are specific, attention getting, written in clear, short, concise, and straightforward language, and printed in large, prominent letters. Warnings also need to be personally relevant. Current U.S. warnings (four rotating messages) do not reflect research since 1984, including information on secondhand smoke, addiction, chemical additives, new findings on disease, and more. We clearly need revamped, up-to-date warning labels. Suggestions—all blunt and to the point—include "Cigarettes kill; one in every three smokers will die from smoking"; "Smoking during pregnancy can harm your baby"; "Cigarettes can kill you"; and "Smoking causes lung cancer."[24]

Stricter regulations on the nicotine content of cigarettes

could also be instituted. Some experts recommend gradually lowering nicotine content to below levels that promote addiction. Such a regulation would keep experimental smokers from becoming addicted. One suggestion is to phase in the nicotine reduction gradually, over ten or fifteen years. While adult (or regular) smokers might compensate for the lower nicotine by smoking more or puffing harder, at least while nicotine levels were still relatively high, such a strategy might help the many who want to quit. It would be easier for them to wean themselves from the nicotine. "When nicotine is low enough, no matter how much people smoke they're not going to be satisfied by it. So I think that eventually they would just give it up," says Neal Benowitz, a proponent of the nicotine reduction strategy.[25]

The Institute of Medicine panel recommends that the federal government authorize a public health agency to prescribe ceilings on levels of tar, nicotine, and other harmful substances in tobacco. The agency would also set policies to discourage tobacco use. One concern, however, is that if nicotine and tar were reduced, consumers might incorrectly believe that tobacco use was safe. Other concerns are that products would have to be carefully monitored for compliance, and that cigarettes with higher levels of nicotine and tar ("high-test" smokes) might be sold on the black market. Thus this is not a simple solution.

CONCLUSION

What a kid decides to do today about smoking can have lifelong consequences. With more than 400,000 Americans dying from smoking-related illnesses every year and kids bombarded from all sides by influences to smoke, our country needs to take a stronger stand on teens and tobacco use. We have done so much to erase so many diseases; surely we should be committed to reducing smoking-related ones as well.

Reducing the teen rate of smoking will be difficult and expensive, requiring dramatic changes in attitudes, regulations, and education. President Clinton's plan—if implemented in some form—may be a significant first step. We'll need commitments on the local, state, and federal levels. But how can we idly stand by as millions of kids play around with a deadly and addictive substance? We need to do whatever we can to help kids see that smoking is not cool or glamorous but a hazard to their present and future well-being.

As one sophomore in high school put it, recalling her first smoke, "I remember sitting there and thinking—I was cool, I'm a rebel. Now, I look back, and I was such a dork."[26] If only kids could learn from others' mistakes.

SOURCE NOTES

1

1. Centers for Disease Control and Prevention, *Preventing Tobacco Use Among Young People: A Report of the Surgeon General* (Washington, D.C.: U.S. Department of Health and Human Services, 1994), introductory letter.

2. John P. Pierce et al., "Trends in Cigarette Smoking in the United States," *Journal of the American Medical Association* 261(1) (1989): 61–65 in Barbara S. Lynch and Richard J. Bonnie, eds., *Growing Up Tobacco Free: Preventing Nicotine Addiction in Children and Youths* (Washington, D.C.: National Academy Press, 1994), 8.

3. *Tobacco-Free Youth Reporter*, Summer 1994, 10; and Barbara S. Lynch and Richard J. Bonnie, *Growing Up Tobacco Free*, 3.

4. Lynch and Bonnie, *Growing Up Tobacco Free*, 3.

5. Ibid.

6. Carl E. Bartecchi, Thomas D. MacKenzie, and Robert W. Schrier, "The Global Tobacco Epidemic," *Scientific American*, May 1995, 46.

7. Lynch and Bonnie, *Growing Up Tobacco Free*, vii.

8. Ibid., 105.

9. Bartecchi et al., "The Global Tobacco Epidemic," 50.

10. Ibid., 47.

11. Centers for Disease Control and Prevention, *Preventing Tobacco Use Among Young People*, iii.

12. Ibid.

13. Shannon Brownlee and Steven V. Roberts, "Should Cigarettes Be Outlawed?," *U.S. News & World Report*, April 18, 1994, 36.

14. Ibid.

15. Bartecchi et al., "The Global Tobacco Epidemic," 46.

16. Ibid.

17. Elizabeth Gleick, "Out of the Mouths of Babes," *Time*, August 21, 1995, 33.

18. Lynch and Bonnie, *Growing Up Tobacco Free*, 7.

19. Bartecchi et al., "The Global Tobacco Epidemic," 46.

20. "Report Describes Global Smoking Epidemic," *Tobacco-Free Youth Reporter*, Spring 1995, 14.

21. Bartecchi et al., "The Global Tobacco Epidemic," 46.

22. Philip Shenon, "Asia's Having One Huge Nicotine Fit," *New York Times*, May 15, 1994, E16.

23. Ibid.

24. John Darnton, "Report Says Smoking Causes a Global Epidemic of Death," *New York Times*, September 21, 1994.

25. Shenon, "Asia's Having One Huge Nicotine Fit," E16.

26. Darnton, "Report Says Smoking Causes a Global Epidemic of Death."

2

1. Barbara S. Lynch and Richard J. Bonnie, eds., *Growing Up Tobacco Free: Preventing Nicotine Addiction in Children and Youths* (Washington, D.C.: National Academy Press, 1994), 8.

2. Robert K. Heimann, *Tobacco and Americans* (New York: McGraw-Hill, 1960), 7.

3. Ibid., 8.

4. Ibid., 34.

5. Ibid., 6.

6. Beryl Brintnall Simpson and Molly Conner-Ororzaly, *Economic Botany: Plants in Our World* (New York: McGraw-Hill, 1986), 408.

7. Gilda Berger, *Smoking Not Allowed: The Debate* (New York: Franklin Watts, 1987), 25.

8. Nancy Day Raines, *Tobacco: Facts for Decisions* (Syracuse, N.Y.: New Reader's Press, 1983), 5.

9. Simpson and Conner-Ororzaly, *Economic Botany*, 411.

10. Berger, *Smoking Not Allowed*, 30.

11. Ibid.

12. Heimann, *Tobacco and Americans*, 53.

13. Ibid., 73.

14. Berger, *Smoking Not Allowed*, 47.

15. Robert Sobel, *They Satisfy: The Cigarette in American Life* (Garden City, N.Y.: Anchor Press/Doubleday, 1978), 6.

16. Ibid., 7.

17. Ibid., 8.

18. Ronald J. Troyer and Gerald E. Markle, *Cigarettes: The Battle Over Smoking* (New Brunswick, N.J.: Rutgers University Press, 1983), 33.

19. Ibid., 40.

20. Ibid.

21. Sobel, *They Satisfy*, 84.

22. Ibid., 85.

23. Ibid., 149.

24. Troyer and Markle, *Cigarettes*, 38.

25. Sobel, *They Satisfy*, 104.

26. Berger, *Smoking Not Allowed*, 68–69.

27. Ibid., 69.

28. Sobel, *They Satisfy*, 190.

29. Ibid., 199.

30. Lynch and Bonnie, *Growing Up Tobacco Free*, 7.

31. Ibid.

32. Editorial, "Smoking's Costs Demand Regulation of Tobacco," *USA Today*, June 21, 1994, 10A.

33. Sobel, *They Satisfy*, 222.

34. Ibid., 235.

35. Lynch and Bonnie, *Growing Up Tobacco Free*, 8.

36. Suein L. Hwang, "Study Links Risk in Teen Smoking to Ad Spending," *Wall Street Journal*, July 21, 1995, B8.

37. "Health Report: The Bad News," *Time*, July 3, 1995, 22.

3

1. Barbara S. Lynch and Richard J. Bonnie, eds., *Growing Up Tobacco Free: Preventing Nicotine Addiction in Children and Youths* (Washington, D.C.: National Academy Press, 1994), 8.

2. Ibid., 45.

3. Ibid.

4. Annette M. La Greca and Edwin B. Fisher Jr., "Adolescent Smoking," *Pediatric Annals* 21(4) (April 1992): 241–250.

5. Centers for Disease Control and Prevention, *Preventing Tobacco Use Among Young People: A Report of the Surgeon General* (Washington, D.C.: U.S. Department of Health and Human Services, 1994), 131.

6. "Hooked on Tobacco: The Teen Epidemic," *Consumer Reports*, March 1995, 145.

7. La Greca and Fisher, "Adolescent Smoking," 241–250.

8. G. Hahn et al., "Adolescents' First and Most Recent Use Situations of Smokeless Tobacco and Cigarettes: Similarities and Differences," *Addictive Behaviors* 15(5) (1990): 439–448 in Centers for Disease Control and Prevention, *Preventing Tobacco Use Among Young People*, 136.

9. K. M. Conrad et al., "Why Children Start Smoking Cigarettes: Predictors of Onset," *British Journal of Addiction* 87(12) (1992): 897–913 in Centers for Disease Control and Prevention, *Preventing Tobacco Use Among Young People*, 130.

10. Lynch and Bonnie, *Growing Up Tobacco Free*, 84.

11. "Hooked on Tobacco: The Teen Epidemic," 142.

12. Steven V. Roberts, "Teens on Tobacco: Kids Smoke for Reasons All Their Own," *U.S. News & World Report*, April 18, 1994, 38.

13. Ibid., 43.

14. Ibid.

15. Nadu Tuakli et al., "Smoking in Adolescence: Methods for Health Education and Smoking Cessation," *Journal of Family Practice* 31(4) (1990): 369–374 in Lynch and Bonnie, *Growing Up Tobacco Free*, 78.

16. Lynch and Bonnie, *Growing Up Tobacco Free*, 79.

17. "Kid Smoking and Suicide," *ASH Smoking and Health Review*, September–October 1994, 6.

18. "Hooked on Tobacco: The Teen Epidemic," 142.

19. Gary Soulsman and Eric Ruth, "Lighting Up Is Cool; Kids Think Quitting Will Be Easy," *Sunday News Journal* (Wilmington, Del.), June 12, 1994, A16.

20. Roberts, "Teens on Tobacco," 43.

128

21. Ibid.

22. "Ex-smoker Syndrome," *University of California, Berkeley, Wellness Letter*, September 1989, 7.

23. Roberts, "Teens on Tobacco," 43.

24. "Ex-smoker Syndrome," 6.

25. Lynch and Bonnie, *Growing Up Tobacco Free*, 152.

26. "Hooked on Tobacco: The Teen Epidemic," 145.

27. Ibid.

28. Lynch and Bonnie, *Growing Up Tobacco Free*, 43.

29. Centers for Disease Control and Prevention, *Preventing Tobacco Use Among Young People*, 30.

30. "Reasons for Tobacco Use and Symptoms of Nicotine Withdrawal Among Adolescent and Young Adult Tobacco Users—United States, 1993," *Morbidity and Mortality Weekly Report* 43(41) (October 21, 1994): 746.

31. Philip J. Hilts, "Is Nicotine Addictive? It Depends on Whose Criteria You Use," *New York Times*, August 2, 1994, C3.

32. "Hooked on Tobacco: The Teen Epidemic," 142.

33. Soulsman and Ruth, "Lighting Up Is Cool; Kids Think Quitting Will Be Easy," A1.

34. "Accessibility of Cigarettes to Youths Aged 12–17 Years—United States, 1989," *Morbidity and Mortality Weekly Report* 41(27) (1992): 485–488.

35. "Hooked on Tobacco: The Teen Epidemic," 146.

36. Centers for Disease Control and Prevention, *Preventing Tobacco Use Among Young People*, 126.

4

1. Centers for Disease Control and Prevention, *Preventing Tobacco Use Among Young People: A Report of the Surgeon General* (Washington, D.C.: U.S. Department of Health and Human Services, 1994), iii.

2. Ibid.

3. Barbara S. Lynch and Richard J. Bonnie, eds., *Growing Up Tobacco Free: Preventing Nicotine Addiction in Children and Youths* (Washington, D.C.: National Academy Press, 1994), 105.

4. Centers for Disease Control and Prevention, *Preventing Tobacco Use Among Young People*, 65.

5. Lynch and Bonnie, *Growing Up Tobacco Free*, 107.

6. Steven V. Roberts, "Teens on Tobacco: Kids Smoke for Reasons All Their Own," *U.S. News & World Report*, April 18, 1994, 43.

7. Stanton A. Glantz, *Tobacco Biology and Politics* (Waco, Tx.: Health ED Co., 1992), 38.

8. "The Surgeon General's First Report for Kids," *SGR 4 Kids (The Surgeon General's Report for Kids About Smoking)*, 1994, 8.

9. Lynch and Bonnie, *Growing Up Tobacco Free*, 111.

10. Ibid.

11. Centers for Disease Control and Prevention, *Preventing Tobacco Use Among Young People*, 112.

12. Lynch and Bonnie, *Growing Up Tobacco Free*, 108.

13. "Tobacco: Does It Have a Future?," *Business Week*, July 4, 1994, 26.

14. "Hooked on Tobacco: The Teen Epidemic," *Consumer Reports*, March 1995, 143.

15. "Joe's Place: The Catalog," *Camel Cash*, Volume 5.

16. Centers for Disease Control and Prevention, *Preventing Tobacco Use Among Young People*, 186.

17. "Hooked on Tobacco: The Teen Epidemic," 145.

18. Roberts, "Teens on Tobacco," 43.

19. Andrew Tobias, *Kids Say Don't Smoke* (New York: Workman Publishing, 1991), np.

20. Lynch and Bonnie, *Growing Up Tobacco Free*, 113.

21. Ibid.

22. A. Blum, "The Marlboro Grand Prix. Circumvention of the Television Ban on Tobacco advertising," *New England Journal of Medicine* 324 (1991): 913–917 in Centers for Disease Control, *Preventing Tobacco Use Among Young People*, 185.

23. "The Surgeon General's First Report for Kids," 9.

24. John Slade, "Teenagers Participate in Tobacco Promotion," *9th World Conference on Tobacco and Health*, 1994 in Lynch and Bonnie, *Growing Up Tobacco Free*, 113.

25. Lynch and Bonnie, *Growing Up Tobacco Free*, 110–111.

26. "The Surgeon General's First Report for Kids," 9.

27. Glantz, *Tobacco Biology and Politics*, 38.

28. Lynch and Bonnie, *Growing Up Tobacco Free*, 117.

29. Centers for Disease Control and Prevention, *Preventing Tobacco Use Among Young People*, 191.

30. Ibid.

31. Ibid.

32. "The Surgeon General's First Report for Kids," 9.

33. Lee Krenis More, "Creator of Ad Admits He was Selling Inclusion," *Ithaca Journal*, April 20, 1994, 10B.

34. *Tobacco-Free Youth Reporter*, Autumn 1994, 15.

35. "What Do They Have in Common?," *Tobacco-Free Youth Reporter*, Summer 1994, 3.

36. Tobias, *Kids Say Don't Smoke*.

37. "More Heroes Smoking in Movies, Study Says," *Ithaca Journal*, June 20, 1994, 2A.

38. Ibid.

39. Ibid.

40. "Hooked on Tobacco: The Teen Epidemic," 144.

5

1. Centers for Disease Control and Prevention, *Preventing Tobacco Use Among Young People: A Report of the Surgeon General* (Washington, D.C.: U.S. Department of Health and Human Services, 1994), 80.

2. L. G. Escobedo et al., "Sports Participation, Age at Smoking Initiation, and the Risk of Smoking Among U.S. High School Students," *Journal of the American Medical Association* 269 (1993): 1391–1395 in Centers for Disease Control and Prevention, *Preventing Tobacco Use Among Young People*, 30.

3. Centers for Disease Control and Prevention, *Preventing Tobacco Use Among Young People*, 30.

4. Carl E. Bartecchi, Thomas D. MacKenzie, and Robert W. Schrier, "The Global Tobacco Epidemic," *Scientific American*, May 1995, 46.

5. "The Surgeon General's First Report for Kids," *SGR 4 Kids (The Surgeon General's Report for Kids About Smoking)*, 1994, 3.

131

6. Janet Raloff, "What's in a Cigarette?," *Science News*, May 21, 1994, 330.

7. Gilda Berger, *Smoking Not Allowed: The Debate* (New York: Franklin Watts, 1987), 71.

8. Doug Levy, "Cigarettes Take a Toll on More Than Lungs and Heart," *USA Today*, July 26, 1994, 5D.

9. Jack E. Henningfield, *Nicotine: An Old-Fashioned Addiction* (New York: Chelsea House, 1986), 124.

10. Ibid., 35.

11. David Krogh, *Smoking, The Artificial Passion* (New York: W. H. Freeman, 1991), 29.

12. Ibid., 30.

13. Henningfield, *Nicotine*, 34.

14. Centers for Disease Control and Prevention, *Preventing Tobacco Use Among Young People*, 24.

15. Ibid., 26–27.

16. W. Y. Craig et al., "Cigarette Smoking-associated Changes in Blood Lipid and Lipoprotein Levels in the 8- to 19-year-old Age Group: a Meta-analysis," *Pediatrics* 85 (1990): 155–158 in Centers for Disease Control and Prevention, *Preventing Tobacco Use Among Young People*, 28.

17. Centers for Disease Control, *Reducing the Health Consequences of Smoking: 25 Years of Progress. A Report of the Surgeon General, Executive Summary* (Washington, D.C.: U.S. Department of Health and Human Services, 1989), 5.

18. Stanton A. Glantz, *Tobacco Biology and Politics* (Waco, Tx.: Health ED Co., 1992), 26.

19. Centers for Disease Control, *Reducing the Health Consequences of Smoking*, 11.

20. Editors of the University of California, Berkeley, *Wellness Letter*, *The Wellness Encyclopedia* (Boston: Houghton Mifflin, 1991), 54.

21. "Female Smokers Have Twice the Lung Cancer Risk," *ASH Smoking and Health Review*, January–February 1994, 6.

22. Centers for Disease Control and Prevention, *Preventing Tobacco Use Among Young People*, 29.

23. "Study Links Pancreatic Cancer to Smoking," *Ithaca Journal*, October 19, 1994, 5A.

24. "Study Links Smoking, Breast Cancer," *Ithaca Journal*, June 4, 1994, 1A.

25. Centers for Disease Control, *Reducing the Health Consequences of Smoking*, 5.

26. Ibid., 21.

27. Glantz, *Tobacco Biology and Politics*, 18.

28. Ibid.

29. Centers for Disease Control and Prevention, *Preventing Tobacco Use Among Young People*, 29.

30. Centers for Disease Control, *Reducing the Health Consequences of Smoking*, 5.

31. Joe Tye, "Protecting Babies From Philip Morris and RJR Nabisco," *Tobacco-Free Youth Reporter*, Spring 1993, 18.

32. Centers for Disease Control, *Reducing the Health Consequences of Smoking*, 5.

33. Berger, *Smoking Not Allowed*, 79.

34. Levy, "Cigarettes Take a Toll on More Than Lungs and Heart," 5D.

35. Glantz, *Tobacco Biology and Politics*, 22.

36. Ibid., 21.

37. Levy, "Cigarettes Take a Toll on More Than Lungs and Heart," 5D.

38. "Smoking Sharply Increases Impotence," *ASH Smoking and Health Review*, January–February 1995, 4.

39. Tye, "Protecting Babies From Philip Morris and RJR Nabisco," 6.

40. Glantz, *Tobacco Biology and Politics*, 21.

41. Tye, "Protecting Babies From Philip Morris and RJR Nabisco," 18.

42. Glantz, *Tobacco Biology and Politics*, 21.

43. Tye, "Protecting Babies From Philip Morris and RJR Nabisco," 6.

44. "Health Report: The Bad News," *Time*, March 20, 1995, 21.

45. Berger, *Smoking Not Allowed*, 87.

46. "Secondhand Smoke: Is It a Hazard?," *Consumer Reports*, January 1995, 31.

47. "EPA Issues Landmark Report on Passive Smoke," *Tobacco-Free Youth Reporter*, Spring 1993, 4.

48. Andrew Tobias, *Kids Say Don't Smoke* (New York: Workman Publishing, 1991).

49. "Secondhand Smoke: Is It a Hazard?," 29.

50. *ASH Smoking and Health Review*, July–August 1994, 6.

51. Ibid.

52. "Secondhand Smoke: Is It a Hazard?," 28.

6

1. Centers for Disease Control and Prevention, *Preventing Tobacco Use Among Young People: A Report of the Surgeon General* (Washington, D.C.: U.S. Department of Health and Human Services, 1994), 162.

2. "Hooked on Tobacco: The Teen Epidemic," *Consumer Reports*, March 1995, 142.

3. "The Real Deal About Tobacco!," *SGR 4 Kids (The Surgeon General's Report for Kids About Smoking)*, 1994, 6.

4. Ibid.

5. Centers for Disease Control and Prevention, *Preventing Tobacco Use Among Young People*, 268.

6. Barbara S. Lynch and Richard J. Bonnie, eds., *Growing Up Tobacco Free: Preventing Nicotine Addiction in Children and Youths* (Washington, D.C.: National Academy Press, 1994), 5.

7. "Smoke-Free Comes at a High Price," *USA Today*, June 9, 1994, 2B.

8. Del Jones and James Cox, "No Tobacco Would Mean Changes for Government," *Ithaca Journal*, June 15, 1994, 10A.

9. Ibid.

10. Philip J. Hilts, "Sharp Rise Seen in Smokers' Health Care Costs," *New York Times*, July 8, 1994, A12.

11. "Health Care Costs," *ASH Smoking and Health Review*, January–February 1994, 6.

12. Hilts, "Sharp Rise Seen in Smokers' Health Care Costs," A12.

13. Ibid.

14. Ibid.

15. Peter Passell, "Economic Scene: Smoking's Economic Cost Isn't a Good Argument for Higher Taxes," *New York Times*, July 14, 1994, D2.

16. Hilts, "Sharp Rise Seen in Smokers' Health Care Costs," A12.

17. Passell, "Economic Scene," D2.

18. Doug Levy, "Dark Victory: Early Deaths Cut Smoking Costs," *USA Today*, July 11, 1994, D1.

19. Ibid.

20. Ibid.

21. Gilda Berger, *Smoking Not Allowed: The Debate* (New York: Franklin Watts, 1987), 114.

22. "Smoke Breaks Take Time," *ASH Smoking and Health Review*, March–April 1994, 7.

23. Del Jones and James Cox, "Economy Would Suffer in Smoke-Free U.S.A.," *Ithaca Journal*, June 14, 1994, 10A.

24. Berger, *Smoking Not Allowed*, 114.

25. Shannon Brownlee and Steven V. Roberts, "Should Cigarettes Be Outlawed?," *U.S. News & World Report*, April 18, 1994, 36.

26. Philip Hilts, "U.S. Sees a Smoking Ban Saving $39 Billion," *New York Times*, April 22, 1994, A9.

27. Mimi Hall and Del Jones, "Cigarette Tax Plan Sparks Hot Protest," *USA Today*, March 10, 1994, 2B.

28. "Smoking and Fires," *ASH Smoking and Health Review*, January–February 1994, 6.

29. Ibid.

30. Tobacco Institute, *The Tax Burden on Tobacco* (Washington, D.C.: Tobacco Institute, 1993) in Lynch and Bonnie, *Growing Up Tobacco Free*, 177.

31. "Teen Cigarette Sales Raise $240 Million in Taxes Each Year," *Spokesman-Review*, February 11, 1994.

32. Robert K. Heimann, *Tobacco and Americans* (New York: McGraw-Hill, 1960), 214.

33. Centers for Disease Control and Prevention, *Preventing Tobacco Use Among Young People*, 265.

34. Ibid.

35. Heimann, *Tobacco and Americans*, 156.

36. Centers for Disease Control and Prevention, *Preventing Tobacco Use Among Young People*, 265.

37. Lynch and Bonnie, *Growing Up Tobacco Free*, 179.

38. Ibid., 178.

39. Ibid., 179.

7

1. Barbara S. Lynch and Richard J. Bonnie, eds., *Growing Up Tobacco Free: Preventing Nicotine Addiction in Children and Youth* (Washington, D.C.: National Academy Press, 1994), 73.

2. Ibid.

3. Ibid.

4. Ibid., 8.

5. SmithKline Beecham, *Gallup Report: A National Survey of Americans Who Smoke* (New York, 1993) in Lynch and Bonnie, *Growing Up Tobacco Free*, 74.

6. Karen Allen et al., "Teenage Tobacco Use: Data Estimates from the Teenage Attitudes and Practices Survey, United States, 1989," *Advance Data* 224: 9 in Lynch and Bonnie, *Growing Up Tobacco Free*, 74.

7. Stanton A. Glantz, *Tobacco Biology and Politics* (Waco, Tx.: Health ED Co., 1992), 42.

8. Ibid.

9. Ibid., 44.

10. Ibid., 46.

11. Centers for Disease Control, *Reducing the Health Consequences of Smoking, 25 Years of Progress: A Report of the Surgeon General, Executive Summary* (Washington, D.C.: U.S. Department of Health and Human Services, 1989), 10.

12. "Doctor's Complaint Helps Smoker's Baby," *ASH Smoking and Health Review*, March–April 1994, 2.

13. Centers for Disease Control, *Reducing the Health Consequences of Smoking . . .*, 10.

14. Brennan Dawson, "Reject This Prohibition," *USA Today*, March 25, 1994, 12A.

15. "Crackdown on Smoking: Are Bans on Tobacco Use Unfair to Smokers?," *Congressional Quarterly Researcher*, December 4, 1992, 1055.

16. Christopher John Farley, "The Butt Stops Here," *Time*, April 18, 1994, 60.

17. "Tobacco: Does It Have a Future?," *Business Week*, July 4, 1994, 28.

18. "School Is In, But Smoking Is Out," *ASH Smoking and Health Review*, September–October 1994, 2.

19. Glantz, *Tobacco Biology and Politics*, 47.

20. Lynch and Bonnie, *Growing Up Tobacco Free*, 90.

21. Ibid.

22. "PepsiCo's Taco Bell Bans Smoking in Its Restaurants," *Wall Street Journal*, March 15, 1994 in Lynch and Bonnie, *Growing Up Tobacco Free*, 91.

23. "ETS: Ongoing Research and Community Response," *Tobacco-Free Youth Reporter*, Autumn 1993, 21.

24. "The 30 Percent Myth," *Consumer Reports*, May 1994, 320.

25. Farley, "The Butt Stops Here," 58.

26. James C. McKinley, Jr., "The Garden Agrees to Curb Cigarette Ads," *New York Times*, April 5, 1995, B3.

27. Betsy Wade, "Smoke-Free Flights Increase," *New York Times*, January 1, 1995, 4 (Travel Section).

28. M. A. Pentz et al., "A Multicommunity Trial for Primary Prevention of Adolescent Drug Abuse," *Journal of the American Medical Association* 261 (1989): 3259–3266 in Centers for Disease Control and Prevention, *Preventing Tobacco Use Among Young People*, 246.

29. Lynch and Bonnie, *Growing Up Tobacco Free*, 88.

30. Ibid., 233.

31. Ibid.

32. Ibid., 234.

33. Shannon Brownlee and Steven V. Roberts, "Should Cigarettes Be Outlawed?," *U.S. News & World Report*, April 18, 1994, 34.

34. Farley, "The Butt Stops Here," 64.

8

1. Shannon Brownlee and Steven V. Roberts, "Should Cigarettes Be Outlawed?," *U.S. News & World Report*, April 18, 1994, 34–35.

2. "Tobacco: Does It Have a Future?," *Business Week*, July 4, 1994, 25.

3. Del Jones and James Cox, "What Would Our Lives Be Like?," *USA Today*, June 9, 1994, 2B.

4. "Tobacco: Does It Have a Future?," 25.

5. Ibid.

6. Allen R. Myerson, "Gone Are the Days When Tobacco Brought Only Wealth," *New York Times*, February 26, 1995, E5.

7. "Regulating Tobacco: Can the FDA Break America's Smoking Habit?," *Congressional Quarterly Researcher*, September 30, 1994, 850.

8. Ibid., 848.

9. Myerson, "Gone Are the Days When Tobacco Brought Only Wealth," 5; Del Jones and James Cox, "No Tobacco Would Mean Changes for Government," *Ithaca Journal*, June 15, 1994, 10A.

10. Mimi Hall and Del Jones, "Cigarette Tax Plan Sparks Hot Protest," *USA Today*, March 10, 1994, 2B.

11. "Fearing Tax Rise Will Cost Jobs, Tobacco Workers Plan a Protest," *New York Times*, March 8, 1994, A19.

12. "Regulating Tobacco: Can the FDA Break America's Smoking Habit?," 844.

13. Jones and Cox, "No Tobacco Would Mean Changes for Government," 10A.

14. "Regulating Tobacco: Can the FDA Break America's Smoking Habit?," 848.

15. Ibid., 853.

16. Jones and Cox, "No Tobacco Would Mean Changes for Government," 10A; Brownlee and Roberts, "Should Cigarettes Be Outlawed?," 34.

17. Brownlee and Roberts, "Should Cigarettes Be Outlawed?," 34.

18. Philip Shenon, "Asia's Having One Huge Nicotine Fit," *New York Times*, May 15, 1994, E16.

19. "Regulating Tobacco: Can the FDA Break America's Smoking Habit?," 847.

20. Shenon, "Asia's Having One Huge Nicotine Fit," E16.

21. Ibid.

22. Ibid.

23. "Tobacco: Does It Have a Future?," 26.

24. Shenon, "Asia's Having One Huge Nicotine Fit," E16.

25. Hall and Jones, 2B.

26. "Regulating Tobacco: Can the FDA Break America's Smoking Habit?," 850.

27. Ibid., 848.

28. Ibid., 852.

29. Ibid.

30. "The Truth About Tobacco, Health and Jobs," *Tobacco-Free Youth Reporter*, Autumn 1993, 20.

31. Andrew Tobias, *Kids Say Don't Smoke* (New York: Workman Publishing, 1991).

32. Philip J. Hilts, "Cigarette Makers Debated the Risks They Denied," *New York Times*, June 16, 1994, D22.

33. Philip J. Hilts, "Method to Produce Safer Cigarette was Found in 60's, but Company Shelved Idea," *New York Times*, May 13, 1994, A20.

34. Brownlee and Roberts, "Should Cigarettes Be Outlawed?," 35.

35. Anastasia Toufexis, "Are Smokers Junkies?," *Time*, March 21, 1994, 62.

36. "Regulating Tobacco: Can the FDA Break America's Smoking Habit?," 857.

37. Deborah Sharp, "Fired Up Fla. Governor Takes On Tobacco Giants," *USA Today*, June 6, 1994, 13A.

38. Richard A. Daynard, "The Third (Tidal) Wave of Tobacco Litigation Begins," *Tobacco-Free Youth Reporter*, Summer 1994, 4.

39. Sharp, "Fired Up Fla. Governor Takes on Tobacco Giants," 13A.

40. Ibid.

41. Daynard, "The Third (Tidal) Wave of Tobacco Litigation Begins," 4.

42. "Tobacco: Does It Have a Future?," 27.

43. Ibid., 28.

44. Ibid., 27.

45. Susan Estrich, "Tobacco's Creed: Money Talks," *USA Today*, May 19, 1994, 13A.

46. Tom Watson, "Election Gives New Hope to Tobacco Growers," *Ithaca Journal*, November 25, 1994, 10A.

47. Joe Urschel, "Congress Plays Politics with Tobacco," *USA Today*, June 6, 1994, 11A.

48. "Tobacco: Does It Have a Future?," 29.

9

1. Philip J. Hilts, "Head of F.D.A. Calls Smoking Pediatric Disease," *New York Times*, March 9, 1995, A22.

2. Gary Soulsman and Eric Ruth, "Lighting Up Is Cool; Kids Think Quitting Will Be Easy," *Sunday News Journal* (Wilmington, Del.), June 12, 1994, A16.

3. Centers for Disease Control and Prevention, *Preventing Tobacco Use Among Young People: A Report of the Surgeon General* (Washington, D.C.: U.S. Department of Health and Human Services, 1994), 230.

4. David M. Murray et al., "Five- and Six-Year Follow-Up Results from Four Seventh-Grade Smoking Prevention Strategies," *Journal of Behavioral Medicine* 12 (1989): 207–218 in Barbara S. Lynch and Richard J. Bonnie, eds., *Growing Up Tobacco Free: Preventing Nicotine Addiction in Children and Youths* (Washington, D.C.: National Academy Press, 1994), 147.

5. Ibid., 152.

6. Ibid., 162.

7. Ibid.

8. Roswell Park Cancer Institute, "Survey of Alcohol, Tobacco and Drug Use Among Ninth Grade Students in Erie County, 1992" in Lynch and Bonnie, *Growing Up Tobacco Free*, 190.

9. "USA Snapshots: Price Might Snuff Smokes," *USA Today*, July 8, 1994, 1.

10. "Is the Smoking Lamp Going Out for Good?," *Business Week*, April 11, 1994, 31.

11. Lynch and Bonnie, *Growing Up Tobacco Free*, 184.

12. Ibid., 192.

13. Geoffrey Cowley, "Taxes as an Antidote to Addiction," *Newsweek*, March 28, 1994, 27.

14. Lynch and Bonnie, *Growing Up Tobacco Free*, 201.

15. Peter Passell, "Economic Scene: Smoking's Economic Cost Isn't a Good Argument for Higher Taxes," *New York Times*, July 14, 1994, D2.

16. Lynch and Bonnie, *Growing Up Tobacco Free*, 211.

17. Ibid., 208.

18. Ibid., 202.

19. Leonard A. Jason et al., "Active Enforcement of Cigarette Control Laws in the Prevention of Cigarette Sales to Minors," *Journal of the American Medical Association* 255 (1991): 3159–3161 in Lynch and Bonnie, *Growing Up Tobacco Free*, 202.

20. Lynch and Bonnie, *Growing Up Tobacco Free*, 209.

21. Ibid., 125.

22. Paul M. Fischer et al., "Recall and Eye Tracking Study of Adolescents Viewing Tobacco Advertisements," *Journal of the American Medical Association* 261 (1989): 84–89 in Lynch and Bonnie, *Growing Up Tobacco Free*, 241.

23. Ibid.

24. Lynch and Bonnie, *Growing Up Tobacco Free*, 243.

25. "Regulating Tobacco: Can the FDA Break America's Smoking Habit?," *Congressional Quarterly Researcher*, September 30, 1994, 855.

26. Shannon Brownlee and Steven V. Roberts, "Should Cigarettes Be Outlawed?," *U.S. News & World Report*, April 18, 1994, 43.

INDEX

accessibility of cigarettes to
teens, 35, 36
addiction to nicotine, 11–13,
34–38, 55, 58–60, 62–63,
98–99, 109–112, 116,
122–123
examples of people with, 8,
26, 58, 73, 75, 102
advertising of cigarettes, 9, 11,
23, 106
bans, 24, 44–45, 88, 121–122
campaigns, 36, 42–43
direct-mail promotions, 47
influence on teens and children, 40–41, 54–55
in magazines, 41, 44
in newspapers, 41, 44
outdoor advertising, 44–45, 122
point-of-sale, 48–49
specialty items, 45–46
at sporting events, 47–48
targeting women, 106
African-American teens smoking
rate, 33
allure of cigarettes, 31
American Cancer Society, 91, 104
Americans for Nonsmokers'
Rights, 90–91, 100
anti-tobacco movement, 22–23

bronchitis, 24, 68, 71

cancer, 9, 37, 50–51, 61, 66–67,
70, 88, 106, 108, 118
lung cancer. *See* lung cancer.
throat cancer, 106
carbon monoxide, 60–61, 65, 69
carcinogens, 60, 71, 72, 92–93
cardiovascular effects of smoking, 64
Centers for Disease Control
(CDC), 77–78
chemical additives in cigarettes, 60
chewing tobacco, 19, 20, 100
chronic obstructive pulmonary
disease (COPD), 68
cigars, 20, 21, 81
class-action suits against tobacco
companies, 110–111
Clinton, Bill, 93, 100, 112,
123–124
consumer-protection laws
exempting tobacco, 97–98
consumption of cigarettes per
U.S. adult, 22

deaths due to smoking, 9, 10, 72

education programs to prevent
smoking, 117–118

Elders, Dr. Joycelyn, 39, 59, 116
emphysema, 24, 50, 61, 66, 68, 88
environmental tobacco smoke
    (ETS). *See* secondhand
    smoke.
Environmental Protection
    Agency (EPA), 92, 93, 111
experimental smoking, 11, 36, 45

fertility problems due to smok-
    ing, 69–70
fire fatalities due to smoking, 10,
    78, 81
Food and Drug Administration
    (FDA), 98–100, 108

health care costs for smoking-
    related illnesses, 72, 77–78
*The Health Consequences of
    Involuntary Smoking*, 91–92
heart disease, 9, 23, 24, 50, 64,
    66, 67–68, 72, 76, 88
high blood pressure, 67–68
high cholesterol, 64, 67–68, 72

impulse buying of cigarettes,
    48–49
influence to smoke by peers and
    siblings, 11, 28, 36
Institute of Medicine, 9, 116,
    119–120, 123
insurance costs for smokers, 76–77

Kessler, David, 98–99, 108, 116
Kids Say Don't Smoke, 43, 50, 87,
    107–108

legal addictive products, ciga-
    rettes as, 13

life expectancy of smoker, 59
long-term health costs of smok-
    ing, 65–71
low-birth-weight babies, 70, 78
lung cancer, 9, 23–24, 65–67, 72,
    84, 88, 91, 93–94, 106, 109,
    114–115

mainstream smoke, 70–71
Marlboro Man, 40, 42, 43, 52, 54

nicotine, 62–63, 69, 72
    addiction. *See* addiction to
        nicotine.
    as anti-depressant, 31
    dependence, 34–35
    level manipulation, 109, 111,
        123
    tolerance, 63
    withdrawal, 35
nonsmokers' rights, 88–92, 100

passive smoking. *See* secondhand
    smoke.
physical fitness effects of smok-
    ing, 64–65
pipes, 15, 17, 19, 20, 81
pregnancy and smoking, 66, 69–70
pressure to smoke, 29, 37
prevalence of smoking miscon-
    ceptions, 30, 39, 44, 54
price of cigarettes, 75, 119
productivity and smoking, 79–80
prohibition of sale of cigarettes, 23

quit-smoking programs, 118

"reasons to smoke," 11, 27–32,
    36, 57–58, 73–74, 114–115

curiosity, 29
depression, 31
insecurity, 11, 57–58
invulnerability, 27, 32
peer acceptance, 11, 28, 36
rebellion, 31
social acceptance, 11, 29–30
stress reduction, 11, 30, 36,
    73–74, 114–115
weight control, 32
regulations for cigarettes,
    122–123
"replacement" smokers, 9
respiratory effects of smoking,
    24, 50, 61–62, 63–64, 68,
    71–72
restaurants as smoke-free, 94–95

secondhand smoke, 10, 70–72,
    78, 90–96, 108, 111, 122
short-term health costs of smok-
    ing, 63–65
sidestream smoke, 70–71
skin problems due to smoking,
    68–69
small-airways lung disease, 50
smoke-free environments, 92–97
Smoke-free Schools Act, 93
snuff, 18, 19, 20
society's view of smoking, 87–88
spittoons, 20, 100
stages of smoking, 35–36
stroke, 67–68, 76

sudden infant death syndrome
    (SIDS), 70

tar, 61–62, 63, 109, 123
tobacco, 14, 15, 16, 18
    anti-tobacco movement,
        22–23
    chewing tobacco, 19, 20, 100
    early critics, 18, 19
    education programs, 117–118
    exemption from consumer
        protection laws, 97–98
    plantations, 18, 19, 107
    regulation, 97–100, 103
    taxes, 19, 81–83, 112
tobacco industry, 9, 40, 47–48,
    81, 87, 91–95, 98, 99,
    103–113
Tobacco Institute, 78–79, 104

Wagner, Honus, 40
warning labels on cigarette pack-
    ages, 65, 69, 109–110, 122
withdrawal from nicotine, 35
women
    as advertising targets, 106
    cancer death rates, 67
    cigarette brands developed
        for, 51–52
    pregnancy and smoking, 66,
        69–70
workplace as smoke-free, 93–94